Brahms: Symphony No. 1

David Brodbeck
Associate Professor of Music, University of Pittsburgh

CAMBRIDGE
UNIVERSITY PRESS

Published by the Press Syndicate of the University of Cambridge
The Pitt Building, Trumpington Street, Cambridge CB2 1RP
40 West 20th Street, New York, NY 10011–4211, USA
10 Stamford Road, Oakleigh, Melbourne 3166, Australia

© Cambridge University Press 1997

First published 1997

Printed in Great Britain at the University Press, Cambridge

A catalogue record for this book is available from the British Library

Library of Congress cataloguing in publication data
Brodbeck, David Lee.
Brahms, Symphony no. 1 / David Brodbeck.
p.   cm. – (Cambridge music handbooks)
Includes bibliographical references
ISBN 0 521 47432 9 (hardback). – ISBN 0 521 47959 2 (paperback).
1. Brahms, Johannes, 1833–1897. Symphonies, no. 1, op. 68, C minor.
I. Title.   II. Series.
ML410.B8B73135   1997
784.2′184–dc20   96–7840   CIP MN

ISBN 0 521 47432 9 hardback
ISBN 0 521 47959 2 paperback

#34517470

for Elisabeth and Katherine

Contents

Plates

Preface

My first serious acquaintance with the subject of this book dates from the fall of 1971. I knew but a handful of "classical" works at that time, but I was friendly with a number of players in the local student orchestra, and, on their invitation, I found myself one day attending a rehearsal of Brahms's C Minor Symphony. Twenty-five years later, I can still recall the powerful impression made on me then by two themes from the opening movement – the haunting oboe solo coming near the end of the slow introduction and the magnificent chorale-like theme that resounds so beautifully in the development. This music literally moved me and, in a very real sense, set into motion the long and deep engagement with the work out of which the present study has emerged.

In the pages that follow I offer an account of the genesis and compositional background of the symphony (Chapters 1 and 2), a detailed discussion of the music (Chapters 3–5), and a brief consideration of the work's early reception (Chapter 6). If I have dwelt at greater length on matters of genesis than have most of the other authors in the series, that is only because Brahms himself struggled with the composition for an unusually long time. The critical reading of the music that forms the core of the book represents the current state of my continuing dialogue, not only with "the work itself," but with its dense network of extra-compositional allusions, in which, as I hope to show, much meaning resides; my approach here, in other words, is more herme- neutic than analytic in nature. The final chapter provides a brief introduction to the issues that mattered most in the early reception-history of the symphony – above all that of the work's relationship to the Beethovenian tradition and its controversial status as "successor" to Beethoven's Ninth.

Serious scholarly attention has come late to Brahms's symphonies, but now it comes in abundance. Reinhold Brinkmann's wide-ranging study of the Second, first published in German in 1990, has recently appeared in a revised English-language version. Soon to follow are two monographic surveys of Brahms's entire symphonic oeuvre, by Walter Frisch and

Raymond Knapp, as well as Robert Pascall's critical edition of the First, prepared as the inaugural volume of the recently launched *Johannes Brahms Gesamtausgabe*.[1] The work of each of these authors has, in one way or another, figured into my own, and I am pleased to add a general word of acknowledgment here.

Research for this book has been supported by a Research Fellowship from the Alexander von Humboldt-Stiftung (Bonn), which permitted me two extensive stays in Germany, as well as by generous grants from the Central Research and Development Fund and the University Center for International Studies of the University of Pittsburgh. Grateful acknowledgment is due to the Staatsbibliothek zu Berlin – Preußischer Kulturbesitz for permission to reproduce the postcard on which Brahms inscribed the earliest version of what later became the "alphorn theme" of the finale; to The Pierpont Morgan Library, New York, for permission to reproduce the last page from the autograph of the symphony, as well as one of the two surviving sketch leaves for the middle movements; and to the Staats- und Universitätsbibliothek Carl von Ossietzky, Hamburg, for permission to publish a transcription of the unpublished letter to Brahms from Adolf Schubring that is quoted in Chapters 5 and 6.

I wish to thank Julian Rushton and Penny Souster for their encouragement of this book (and for their forbearance in the face of unexpected delays in its completion). Walter Frisch kindly read the entire manuscript and offered a number of helpful comments, for which I am most grateful. Likewise deserving of thanks are a number of other individuals who have shown an interest in this project and helped in various ways: Styra Avins, Daniel Beller-McKenna, George Bozarth, Hermann Danuser, Kurt Hofmann, Alan Krueck, and Michael Struck.

To Gustav Abel, president of the Baden-Baden Brahmsgesellschaft, I am indebted for his kind invitation to spend two unforgettable weeks during the summer of 1995 at the *Brahmshaus* in Lichtental, where, living and working in the very space in which Brahms had completed his symphony, I was able nearly to finish my typescript. Finally, I wish to acknowledge here the loving encouragement and support of Leonora Saavedra, my companion in Lichtental and partner in so much else during our beautiful project together.

---

[1]   Reinhold Brinkmann, *Johannes Brahms, Die Zweite Symphonie, Späte Idylle* (Munich, 1990); revised and translated as *Late Idyll: The Second Symphony of Johannes Brahms*, trans. Peter Palmer (Cambridge, Mass., 1995); Walter Frisch, *Brahms: The Four Symphonies* (New York: Schirmer, in press); Raymond Knapp, *Brahms and the Challenge of the Symphony* (New York: Pendragon, in press); Johannes Brahms, *Symphonie Nr. 1 c-Moll opus 68*, ed. Robert Pascall (Munich: G. Henle-Verlag, 1996).

Frustrated efforts

After Haydn writing a symphony was no longer a joke but rather a matter of life and death.[1]

Brahms was forty-three years old when, in November 1876, his long-awaited First Symphony was finally given to the world. Widely recognized by then as one of the leading composers of the day, Brahms had demonstrated his mastery in virtually every significant genre apart from opera. Yet the symphony stood as a looming exception. For more than two decades he had grappled with the genre, but an appropriate realization had always eluded him. In 1854 he worked in vain on a Symphony in D Minor (parts of which survive in the First Piano Concerto and *German Requiem*), and five years later he made a reluctant (and unsuccessful) effort to transform the First Serenade into a Symphony in D Major. These early failed attempts had taught Brahms to fear the deep water, and, despite the continual encouragement of his friends and the ever growing expectations of the public, he simply could not be rushed into taking the plunge for a third time.

Indeed, the Symphony in C Minor represents an effort that was spread over many years. A draft of the opening Allegro was in hand by 1862, but the work then evidently was laid aside for more than a decade and did not attain its definitive form until 1877. Unfortunately, precious few musical sources by which to follow Brahms's compositional process have been preserved. No autograph of the first movement survives, and the complete Andante exists only in a fair copy that reflects significant changes that were made after a run of trial performances during the season of 1876–7.[2] The scherzo and finale do come down to us in revealing autographs that were used as the conductor's score in some of these early hearings, but they too document only later stages in the complicated delivery.[3]

The earlier stages of the compositional process are even less well documented. Suggestive clues, none the less, may be found within the symphony's typically dense web of allusions. The most obvious source was

Beethoven, whose mark can be seen in the work's narrative of *per aspera ad astra*, tracing a path from stormy opening movement (whose tonality and "fateful" rhythmic motif come straight from Beethoven's Fifth) to triumphant finale (whose main theme echoes the *Freudenthema* of the Ninth). Yet, as I shall argue in later chapters, certain less obvious allusions to music by Robert Schumann and J. S. Bach, appearing likewise in the outer movements, may provide more crucial evidence bearing on the protracted genesis of the work. But if we are to make any sense of Brahms's great difficulties, we must begin with the circumstances of his extraordinary debut.

First attempts

In his famous essay "Neue Bahnen," published in the *Neue Zeitschrift für Musik* on 28 October 1853, Robert Schumann took pointed aim at the editorial stance of his successor at the journal, Franz Brendel. Since taking over the helm eight years earlier, Brendel had become increasingly vocal in his advocacy of Wagnerian opera and the new program music of Liszt and his followers in Weimar. To Schumann, however, the *Zukunftsmusiker* who drew so much attention from Brendel counted for nothing; he placed his hopes for the future instead on a number of more traditional composers in his own circle. In a promising body of works by artists such as Joseph Joachim, Albert Dietrich, and Woldemar Bargiel, Schumann had seen the announcement of an impending "new musical force," and now, he enthused, that force had suddenly arrived in the person of an obscure young musician named Johannes Brahms. Here was a veritable Messiah, who had been "called to articulate in an ideal way the highest expression of the time." Already Brahms had written "veiled symphonies" for piano, songs "whose poetry one could understand without knowing the words," and even a host of impressive chamber works, and surely, as Schumann prophesied, he would someday "lower his magic wand where the powers of the masses in the choir and orchestra can lend him their strength" and so present "still more wonderful glimpses into the mysteries of the spirit-world."[4]

This hope for a truly grand work from Brahms – for a worthy successor to Beethoven's Ninth, we might say – found even clearer expression in Schumann's letter to Joachim of 6 January 1854: "Now, where is Johannes? ... Is he not yet allowing timpani and drums to resound? He should always recall the beginnings of Beethoven's symphonies; he should seek to make something similar. The beginning is the main thing; once one has begun, the end comes to him as if by itself."[5] And to judge from the opening Maestoso of the Piano Concerto in D Minor, Op. 15, which can be traced back to material that dates from this early period, Brahms did not at first back away from the challenge. With timpani resounding, the concerto begins with a reinterpretation of the first pages of Beethoven's Ninth – although in Brahms's hands the dramatic and suspenseful process of the model unfolds breathlessly in only a few measures' time. Whereas Beethoven gradually (and inexorably) develops from tonally ambiguous fifths a well-formed theme that arpeggiates the tonic, and only then, in a varied repetition, leads unexpectedly to an arpeggiation of B♭, Brahms, in a sudden dramatic burst, lets loose at once with his plunge through the submediant.

The Ninth Symphony did not stand alone in Brahms's thoughts, however. We have it on Joachim's word that the opening measures of the concerto originated "in the visualization of Schumann's suicide attempt" on 27 February 1854,[6] and echoes of the outer movements of Schumann's own D Minor Symphony, Op. 121, surely can be heard, too. From its first movement comes the very timpani roll that calls Brahms's piece into life as well as a model for the unusual "gapped" structure of his arpeggiated main theme; from the slow introduction to Schumann's finale comes a similar odd combination of pedal point on D, first-inversion harmony on B♭, and tonally ambiguous arpeggiated theme.

Although these allusions to the last published symphonies of both his revered hero and beloved benefactor are suggestive of Brahms's high ambitions for the piece, his ideas originally took shape, not in a concerto or in any other orchestral dress, but in a Sonata for Two Pianos. The first three movements, which, significantly, were written at around the time when Brahms heard the Ninth Symphony for the first time, came easily and were finished by early April 1854.[7] Brahms was far from satisfied with the music, however, and on 19 June 1854 he announced to Joachim: "I wish I could leave my D Minor Sonata alone for a long while. I've often played the first three movements with Frau Schumann. (Improved.) To tell the truth, I require even more than two pianos."[8] Indeed, with the aid of his friend Julius Otto Grimm, Brahms soon produced a symphonic transcription of the first movement, which he sent for Joachim's inspection on 27 July.[9]

The example of Schubert's Duo Sonata for Piano in C Major, D. 812, could not have been far from his mind. This *Grand Duo*, after all, was the work that Schumann had long suspected of being a piano arrangement of a symphony and about which he had written, in words echoing those cited above, that "one hears string and wind instruments, tuttis, solo passages, timpani-rolls; the broad symphonic form, even echoes of … Beethoven's

3

symphonies." And it was to Joseph Joachim's orchestration of this work that Brahms was referring when in the following year he mentioned a certain "Schubertsche Sinfonie" to Clara Schumann. It is hard, then, to resist concluding that in his own Duo Sonata the composer had planned from the start to make a "Brahms'sche Sinfonie."[10]

At all events, it is not surprising, in view of the probable role played by Beethoven's Ninth in the conception of the work, that Brahms progressed slowly, if at all, on the finale. Thus no mention was made of any last movement when on 30 January 1855 the young composer finally mustered the courage to announce the piece to Schumann: "By the way, I spent all last summer trying to write a symphony; the first movement was even orchestrated, and the second and third composed. (In D minor $\frac{6}{4}$ slow)." Borrowing gestures from Beethoven's tragic opening movement was one thing, but emulating his choral finale – and, as Christopher Reynolds has argued, Brahms might well have intended to do just that – was something else again.[11] The Beethovenian model – with its great length and complex form, its thematic recollections, recitatives, and choral setting of the "Ode to Joy" – was in every respect daunting. Yet only a few days after reporting to Schumann about the piece Brahms saw a way out of his dilemma. He dreamt that he had used two parts of his "hapless symphony," as he described the piece to Clara Schumann on 7 February 1855, in a piano concerto, consisting of "the first movement and scherzo with a finale, terribly difficult and grand." Thus was the symphony abandoned and its first movement, indeed, eventually revised as the opening Maestoso of the First Piano Concerto.[12]

If "Neue Bahnen" forms an indispensable part of the context in which to understand the aborted Symphony in D Minor, then Brahms's next orchestral work, the Serenade in D, Op. 11, must finally be seen against the backdrop formed by Franz Brendel's belated rejoinder to Schumann's essay. On 10 June 1859 the *Neue Zeitschrift* led with the editor's inaugural address to the first *Tonkünstlerversammlung* of what later became the *Allgemeiner Deutscher Musikverein*. Here Brendel proposed replacing the expression "Music of the Future" with "New German School," which he held was led by Wagner, Liszt, and Berlioz, and which represented, in a kind of synthesis of historical periods, the "entire post-Beethoven development."[13] Brahms, who knew at first hand the problem of following in the steps of Beethoven, and who had by then come to very different terms with the Baroque and Classical past, responded angrily. In August 1859 he reported to Joachim that "his fingers often itched to start a fight, to write something anti-Liszt."

Significantly, it was the recent orchestral works of the Weimar master – the *Dante* Symphony and newly published symphonic poems – that Brahms singled out for scorn, likening them to so many contagions in a spreading "plague." And for that reason it is scarcely surprising that his contemporaneous First Serenade plays like something "anti-Liszt."[14]

This stylistic orientation is apparent from the very beginning. Brahms not only ignores Brendel's "post-Beethoven development" but, so to speak, retreats to a "pre-Beethoven" era. Here, as many early reviewers were quick to observe, the composer virtually quotes the beginning of the finale to Haydn's "London" Symphony. He begins, that is, at the point in history at which Beethoven himself had begun, with the last movement of Haydn's final essay in the genre. As the piece unfolds, references to other "healthy" models follow in abundance, ranging from Beethoven's Septet to Schumann's Second Symphony. And echoes of Beethoven symphonies are to be heard, too; but these are of the Second and Sixth Symphonies, not, tellingly, the Ninth.[15]

In view of the larger context in which the serenade was written – considering both Brahms's struggle (and desire) to compose a symphony and his horror at the evident advance of Liszt's new orchestral paradigms – it is understandable that he finally reworked the piece. In its first incarnation, which was shared with friends in the summer of 1858, the piece consisted of four movements only and was scored for a chamber ensemble consisting of flute, clarinet, horn, bassoon, and strings. From the start, there was talk that the piece should be converted into a symphony, as we can infer from Joachim's letter of October 1858: "Without hearing it I shouldn't like to help in deciding whether you really should set the serenade for orchestra, or perhaps only add another horn and oboe. In any case, the piece has 'symphony' written all over it" (*ist ... sehr Sinfonie-verkündend*). Yet Brahms refused to "break with the original instrumentation," as Joachim explained to Clara Schumann, and at the end of the year actually made the work seem less like a symphony by adding two scherzi. In this six-movement form the piece was first played publicly, on 28 March 1859, by a "small orchestra" of Hamburg musicians led by Joachim.[16] Brahms remained dissatisfied, however, and on 8 December 1859 he asked his friend to return the score and to include with it some music paper in a large format. "I need the paper," he wrote with a certain sense of resignation, "in order finally to turn the First Serenade into a symphony. The work is a kind of mongrel, I see, nothing is right. I had such beautiful, great ideas for my first symphony, and now!"[17] Brahms was less candid to Karl Bargheer, the first violinist in the

5

Detmold orchestra, who interrupted him one day at work. As Max Kalbeck related the story:

Bargheer surprised him ... at noon. Everything in his room, piano, bed, table and chair, was covered with leaves of full score [*Partiturbogen*], which Brahms, who was accustomed to rising very early, had filled with writing in the morning. "I am setting the Serenade for orchestra," he said; "it will be much better." When Bargheer asked him whether then it would be a symphony, Brahms expressed his opinion that "If one wants to write symphonies after Beethoven, then they will have to look very different!"[18]

Notwithstanding this disavowal, the orchestral score that Brahms produced originally was headed "Sinfonie-Serenade"; and it was this designation that Joachim used when he recorded his great happiness upon receiving the work at Christmas 1859 and again two months later, when requesting both score and parts for a forthcoming rehearsal of the new version. Yet when Brahms complied with this request he expressed his final view of the work in no uncertain terms: "Here come the score and parts to the D Major *Serenade*, if I may."[19] Again it had come to naught: if the abandoned D Minor Symphony had leaned too far toward Beethoven's Ninth, the erstwhile "Sinfonie-Serenade" must have seemed overly inclined in the opposite direction.

Contexts for the opening Allegro

It remains a mystery when Brahms set to work on what finally became the First Symphony. Evidently the first person to lay eyes on the music was the composer's friend Albert Dietrich, with whom Brahms passed a holiday in June 1862. In his memoirs Dietrich recalled that "in Münster am Stein Brahms ... showed me the first movement of his C Minor Symphony, which however appeared only later and considerably revised." Elsewhere, addressing Max Kalbeck's question of whether Brahms had composed the movement during that summer, Dietrich gave critical evidence regarding both the comparatively early date of the piece and the nature of the composer's subsequent revisions: "The first movement of the C Minor Symphony *was already finished* in Münster am Stein, though it lacked the slow introduction." But as for when this opening Allegro might actually have been written, Dietrich was unable to provide any clues whatsoever.[20]

For his part, Kalbeck conjectured that the first movement originated in the emotionally troubled year of 1855. Just as Robert Schumann's suicide attempt in February 1854 and Brahms's first live experience of Beethoven's Ninth in the following month had, in his view, given rise to the ill-fated Symphony in D Minor, so he reasoned that the composer's hopeless love for Clara Schumann (which was in full bloom by early 1855) and his initial experience at that very time of Robert Schumann's incidental music to Byron's *Manfred* (whose protagonist is driven to guilt and despair over an incestuous love) form the soil in which the first movement of the C Minor Symphony "began . . . to germinate." Indeed, encouraged by a similarity between the second theme of Brahms's opening Allegro and a passage from the development of the second theme in the *Manfred* Overture, Kalbeck suggested that the first movement could be understood autobiographically as depicting "the relations between Johannes, Robert, and Clara."[21]

Kalbeck's authority on this matter has often been challenged. But, to be fair, we should note that he in fact hedged on the question of whether Brahms actually wrote any music for the symphony in 1855, holding only that the work's "germ" (which I take to mean something like "source of inspiration") dated from that year.[22] And though the biographer did not choose the best musical example with which to carry the point, his speculation regarding the music's autobiographical basis – his provocative account of the work in terms of the intense Oedipal drama in which Brahms was entangled during the mid-1850s – does find support, as we shall discover in Chapter 3, in the existence of a network of salient allusions to a number of works by Schumann, including both *Manfred* and the Fourth Symphony.

But these same allusions may also point to a second, somewhat later stimulus to composition, one involving not only autobiography, but the continuing ideological struggle of the day concerning the historical roles played Beethoven and Schumann and the merits of the *Zukunftsmusik*. This struggle came to a head in the spring of 1860, when Brahms and Joachim decided finally to act on their desire to go public in opposition to Liszt and the New German School. In March of that year Brahms not only thanked Joachim for sending a draft of such a written protest but reported on his own efforts to enlist fellow musicians who might be expected to join their cause. Joachim, in turn, suggested that additional support might be found at the forthcoming Lower Rhine Music Festival ("this national meeting of praise-worthy musicians," as he put it), which was to be held in Düsseldorf on 27–9 May 1860.[23]

Soon thereafter, however, the violinist reported that Clara had been invited to a rather different gathering, to be held in Zwickau on 7–8 June 1860 in commemoration of the fiftieth anniversary of her late husband's birth. The widow had no interest in attending this "Erinnerungsfeier," Joachim explained, because "the participation of the Weimarites would have contradicted too much the wishes of her Robert."[24] (In the public announcement of the Zwickau festival, which appeared in Brendel's *Neue Zeitschrift* and appealed for the participation of all who "had personally stood near to the immortal Master," the matter was put more tactfully: "Frau Clara Schumann, whose participation had to be the Committee's first task to win, has shown her lively interest in the festival, to be sure, but has declined to participate."[25]) Meanwhile, even as Brahms and Joachim continued to revise their "Manifesto" and solicit the support of others, a copy fell into enemy hands. On 4 May an anonymous parody by Carl Friedrich Weitzmann ran in the *Neue Zeitschrift*; two days later, the text itself appeared in the *Berliner Musik-Zeitung Echo*, with the names of only Brahms, Joachim, Grimm, and Bernhard Scholz underneath.[26] News traveled slowly, however, and on 15 May Joachim reported in all innocence that Julius Rietz and several other musicians had agreed to join the protest, provided that "the blow" be deferred until after the Zwickau festival, at which, it was thought, a "provocation" would surely arise. And yet another week passed before Joachim learned of the premature publication and sent word of it to his colleague in Hamburg.[27]

Brahms, traveling with Frau Schumann, met Joachim in Düsseldorf to discuss this unwelcome development, and from there, bypassing Zwickau, the party continued on finally to Bonn.[28] In his report on the "Erinnerungsfeier," appearing on 15 June 1860, Brendel pointedly took note of the three conspicuous absences, while seizing the opportunity to escalate the recent war of words:

If something of a shadow was cast on the otherwise unclouded festival, it was the observation that some of Schumann's special friends and admirers had not come ... [T]here is now a little circle of Schumann's admirers which seems to want to take his cult as its private possession ... The unquestionable one-sidedness that is implied by this, which is intensifying to the point of becoming pathological, is quite apparent, and no impartial person will agree with this faction if it maintains that the spaces in the temple of art are so limited that there is room only for itself and Schumann.[29]

In this heavy atmosphere both Joachim and Clara encouraged Brahms to work. Thus the violinist's next letter, written toward the end of June begins: "You too are completely silent! Hopefully you are speaking a lot to yourself [*viel monologisiert*], in tones." Even more suggestive is Clara's letter of 21 June: "I am being thoroughly lazy but feel that is having a bad effect on me and from now on want to be busy again. I hope very much that you are too and are working quietly in your little ground-floor room. People like you take in Nature's charms everywhere and thereby create nourishment for their spirit ... *A fine stormy sky can in this way pass into a symphony – who knows what already happened!?*"[30]

It is important in this context to recall that Brahms was a self-described *Wagnerianer*; his quarrel, as he had made clear to Joachim when the two were working out the final text of the Manifesto, was not with Wagner (or even Berlioz) but only with Liszt's music and the editorial policies of Brendel's *Neue Zeitschrift*. Thus it seems probable that Brahms would have sought out Wagner's much discussed, eagerly anticipated *Tristan und Isolde* when it was published in early 1860; with that in mind, Robert Fink has even suggested that the chromatic motto of Brahms's opening Allegro (mm. 38–42) can be related – whether as "a conscious allusion, unconscious influence, or just a fortuitous convergence of expressive resources" – to the chromatically charged opening of the *Tristan* Prelude.[31] Moreover, in view of the same experiences in Brahms's personal life that Kalbeck related to Schumann's *Manfred*, we can easily imagine that Brahms would have responded to the "message" of Wagner's prelude. As Richard Pohl put it, in a review that Brahms undoubtedly read of a concert in June 1859 that included both the *Manfred* Overture and the still unpublished Prelude to *Tristan*, here Wagner gives perfect expression to "the genuinely human struggling and atoning hero, who revels in the consuming passions of a forbidden love and perishes, yet who even in his moments of highest rapture is shudderingly consumed by the demonic proximity of an invisibly controlling nemesis."[32]

The genesis of the First Symphony, to be sure, remains shrouded in uncertainty. But if the seeds had been sown amid the traumatic events of the mid-1850s, they might well have sprouted during the troubled time surrounding the Manifesto and Schumann festival. For in the powerful opening Allegro of his First Symphony, as we shall see, Brahms not only addressed issues that had been raised in Wagner's latest score but staked his claim to precisely what Brendel would have denied him – to be the privileged executor of Schumann's musical estate.[33]

"Symphony by J. B.?"

Brahms showed the completed first movement to Dietrich, as we have seen, at Münster am Stein in June 1862. Clara Schumann, who was living nearby that summer and thus saw a good deal of both men, read through the score soon after Dietrich had examined it. This development she reported to Joachim in a letter of 1 July:

Johannes recently sent me – think what a surprise – a symphonic first movement, with the following bold opening:

That is rather audacious perhaps, but I have quickly become used to it. The movement is full of wonderful beauties, with a mastery in the treatment of the motifs which is indeed becoming more and more characteristic of him. Everything is so interestingly interwoven, yet as spirited as a first outburst; one enjoys [it] so completely to the full, without being reminded of the craft. In the transition from the second part back to the first he has once more succeeded splendidly.[34]

No sooner had Brahms revealed the promising piece, however, than did he shelve it and turn his attention to another project. As he explained to Dietrich at the beginning of September, just before departing on his momentous first visit to Vienna: "the symphony is not yet ready, unlike a string quintet ... in F minor, which I would really like to send you and have you write about it to me, but I suppose I had better take it with me."[35] Later that month Joachim pressed the composer for information regarding the piece, which he hoped to perform in the following season. But it was his new chamber work, which some years later took shape as the Piano Quintet in F Minor, Op. 34, that Brahms sent in response to his friend's letter of inquiry, not the orchestral movement, about which he laconically wrote, "after 'Symphony by J. B.' you may place a ?."[36]

As for the new quintet, its symphonic scope was unmistakable. Thus Clara Schumann noted in her reaction to Brahms's subsequent revision of the piece as a sonata for two pianos (which later appeared as Op. 34*bis*): "it is no sonata but rather a work whose ideas you could – you must – scatter over the entire orchestra as if from a horn of plenty! ... Right from the first time I played it [as a string quintet] I had the feeling of its being an arrangement."[37] Indeed, if the final versions of the symphonic Allegro and quintet are any indication, the one must have echoed in Brahms's mind as he worked on the other. The scherzo of Op. 34, for example, not only stands in the same $\frac{6}{8}$ meter and key of C minor as the scherzo-like symphonic first movement but, in the passage that is first heard in measures 23–30, recalls the beautiful chorale-like theme (and background triplet accompaniment) from the earlier work's development (mm. 232–6). By the same token, the expressive chromatic ascents heard repeatedly in the slow introduction to the quintet's finale bring to mind the opening measures of the symphonic Allegro, whose chromatic second theme (mm. 130ff.) likewise resonates in the second group of the finale of the quintet (mm. 94ff.).

Why did Brahms once more abandon a symphony and channel his ideas into a less threatening genre instead? Practical considerations must be given their due. The composer was about to embark for Vienna and surely would have desired bringing along another large and serious new chamber work to use in impressing the Viennese public. But there can be little doubt that as a symphonist Brahms remained encumbered by the imposing example of Beethoven. Indeed, as Raymond Knapp has suggested, the composer's preoccupation during the years 1863–71 with works for chorus and orchestra, including *Rinaldo*, *Ein deutsches Requiem*, the *Alto Rhapsody*, the *Schicksalslied*, and the *Triumphlied*, might even indicate that he was continuing to entertain thoughts of composing a choral symphony of his own.[38]

In limbo

Although Brahms received a number of inquiries about the symphony throughout this productive period – its existence soon became an open secret among his friends – his responses (such as they are) tell us next to nothing. Persistent queries from Clara Schumann (November 1863 and January 1864), Hermann Levi (November 1864 and February 1865), and Adolf Schubring (September 1866 and February 1869) seem to have gone unanswered, and when Brahms did speak about the piece – to Julius Stockhausen in the spring of 1864 (who learned of its "somewhat décolleté condition") and Albert Dietrich in September 1866 ("I cannot wait upon you with a symphony") – he was scarcely forthcoming about his progress.[39]

Levi, to whom Brahms was especially close during these years, held one of the best positions from which to judge how far work on the piece had advanced. Yet in his letter of 3 May 1870 the conductor had to resort to this friendly jibe: "What I'd really like to hear from you – the form in which the products of your industrious winter have taken, whether you have required a lot of music paper, especially of the 16-stave variety in which the flutes stand at the top – I'd just rather not inquire about; in the first place I deserve no answer, and in the second I shouldn't get one even if I did deserve it."[40] Thus it is not surprising that Max Bruch, a mutual acquaintance of both men, received no word of the piece in response to a similar inquiry that he sent only three days later: "What will you bring us next? I'm very anxious. Perhaps an opera? Or a symphony? You should finally resolve to realize your symphonic sketches!" Brahms answered instead with an inquiry of his own concerning the position of Kapellmeister that Bruch was vacating in Sonderhausen. In his reply, dated 15 June 1870, Bruch glowed about the fine court orchestra and, as an enticement, added that performances of new orchestral works were common: "The Ninth Symphony, Schumann's works (why can't I add 'the Brahms symphonies!')"; then, inviting Brahms to visit in order to hear for himself, he added: "It would be wonderful if you decided to rehearse your 'symphony movements' with us."[41]

The appearance of Bruch in our narrative is significant and calls for a brief digression, not only to evaluate his testimony with regard to the state of Brahms's symphony at the time but also to examine critical evidence concerning broader matters of symphonic style and compositional aspiration. Like most conservative musicians of the day, Bruch had been awaiting a symphony from Brahms for some time. "What is he doing, and where is he hiding?" he inquired of Levi already on 6 December 1866, adding "When you write to Brahms, greet him heartily ... and urge him to write a great, splendid symphony, which will directly strike the hearts of the people, and shake and jolt the philistines so that they will not know what hit them!"[42] Yet judging from Bruch's remarks of only seven weeks later, he was not yet convinced that Brahms was really capable of producing such a piece:

A vocal work is created under completely different conditions from an instrumental work; a choral work which intends to *make its effect* with masses and through masses, must do without excessive refinement of workmanship. Since for some years I have responsibly put the *main* emphasis on the *melody*, it has for that reason been impossible for me to apply the same attention to instrumental filigree-work. And what I have too little of, Brahms has too much of; he takes such an unending joy in everything that one calls workmanship and contrapuntal niceties that, perhaps as a result, a *pregnant melody* is lacking in his things – most of his things are melodic in the noble sense but not always pregnant.[43]

Levi came to a rather different conclusion when making his own comparison between the styles of the two composers. In his letter to Bruch of 11 February 1867 he openly criticized his friend's Violin Concerto in G

Minor for having no real thematic development and continued: "What you lack can be seen in all the places in your vocal works in which the musical invention isn't able to proceed directly from the words, in all the preludes, postludes, interludes ... From a beautiful improvisation to a beautiful artwork is an even bigger step. To curb his improvising, to banish it from his artistic form – that's what makes the master."[44]

Responding to criticism of this sort, Bruch announced on 30 March 1868 that he had recently sketched a symphony, adding "I have laid much emphasis on thematic development." Two weeks later, recounting with understandable pride the success with which the new concerto had been greeted by the public, he elaborated: "In the meanwhile I am free to make a symphony. The concerto has given me the courage to write instrumental music, although you once thought I lacked [a talent] for it. In the symphony you shall find all the development that is not in the concerto and which is not needed there."[45] Levi was still skeptical, however; he not only encouraged Bruch to "try for once to forget that Mendelssohn and Schumann lived, to link directly onto Bach and Beethoven," but suggested that he would do well to take Brahms as a model. This last bit of advice was the cause of some annoyance, and on 26 April 1868 Bruch replied testily that the listeners of his concerto "are not astonished from a cold distance as with many works of *your* god [i.e., Brahms] but rather are pleased by it in the *heart*."[46]

Remarkably enough, the piece that Bruch seems to have had closest in mind here was not one of Brahms's instrumental compositions but his great *German Requiem*. Writing to Ferdinand Hiller on the same day as to Levi, he admitted that this choral–orchestral work, whose triumphant première he had attended at Bremen Cathedral on 10 April 1868, "makes a meaningful impression not only on artists, but also on the people," and added that "Brahms has, so it seems, achieved something here that was hitherto denied to him"; yet, as he continued, "for all that I believe that one will feel toward this work more respect, admiration, than love. I am frank enough to say that to me a powerful ravishing melody is preferable to the most magnificent imitations and contrapuntal tight-rope walking."[47]

Bruch's reservations about Brahms's style did not, however, prevent a warm friendship from springing up between the two composers when they met for the first time that summer at the Lower Rhine Music Festival in Cologne. Indeed, when at the end of the year Bruch published his Symphony No. 1 in E♭, Op. 28, he dedicated it to the very composer whom he had recently disparaged, forwarding the score on 22 December 1868 with these words: "By adorning my work with your name, dear Brahms, I wish above all to demonstrate to you how highly as an aspiring comrade-in-art I treasure your ability and accomplishments, how very much I enjoy and admire your truly significant and ever increasing power of production."[48]

Brahms immediately thanked Bruch for the dedication but evidently did not write again until 21 February 1870, when he reported cordially about the Viennese première of the symphony at the Philharmonic under the baton of its director, Otto Dessoff:

In spite of my fear of [writing] paper, I cannot refrain from thanking you with a few words for the symphony, which we heard here yesterday. On my way out and in the course of the day I spoke with a rather large number of critics. Now, you know how these [types] love to associate with us, their charges; since you seem nevertheless to be interested more than I in everything having to do with performances, then I wouldn't like the caressings of these men to be the only news this time. The symphony really went quite splendidly – in every way. Every movement without exception was applauded. The scherzo in particular had quite an extraordinary success, which was owing not only to the piece but also to the brilliant spirited performance ... With much joy (and some envy) I see how busy and hardworking you are.[49]

The ending of this last letter anticipates a rather more candid and revealing statement that Brahms made two months later to his publisher Fritz Simrock, who was set already to release Bruch's Symphony No. 2 in F Minor, Op. 36: "I congratulate you regarding Bruch's symphony; hopefully I will be properly envious of it when I see it. As usual, I am always surprised less that I am so lazy than that others can be so industrious."[50]

These remarks raise once more the question of how Brahms's own symphony stood in early 1870. It is clear from our survey of the correspondence that Bruch had not obtained his information about the piece at first hand; perhaps it had come from Levi, but even he, as we have seen, actually knew very little. At any rate, the casual and imprecise choice of Bruch's locutions is self-evident – what were described as "sketches" in May 1870 had become "movements" by the following month – and it seems doubtful that Brahms had yet proceeded very far beyond the first movement. In short, except for an early version of the famous "alphorn theme" of the finale – which was conceived as a birthday greeting for Clara Schumann in September 1868 and sent from Switzerland on a card headed "Also blus das Alphorn heut" and inscribed with the text "Hoch auf'm Berg, tief im Thal, grüß' ich dich viel tausendmal!" ("Thus blew the alphorn today: High in the mountains, deep in the valley, I greet you a thousand times over.") – there simply is no trace from the 1860s of more than the opening Allegro

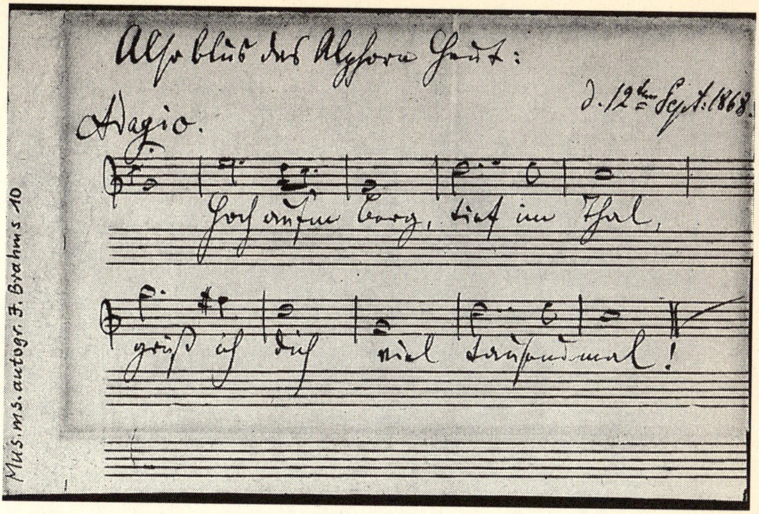

Plate 1.1 Postcard from Brahms to Clara Schumann, 12 September 1868, with the first version of the "alphorn theme" of the finale. Staatsbibliothek zu Berlin – Preußischer Kulturbesitz.

(Plate 1.1).[51] And when the next decade began, the prospect of ever completing a work that would be worthy of Beethoven must have seemed remote. As Brahms put it in a well-known remark to Levi that probably dates from their meeting in Karlsruhe in October 1871: "I will never compose a symphony! You have no idea how it feels to one of us when he continually hears behind him such a giant."[52]

Completion, first performances, and publication

My symphony is long and not exactly charming.[1]

Ironically, Brahms's resigned acceptance of his defeat as a symphonist came at the very time when he was experiencing his first widespread successes as a composer. Indeed, the *German Requiem*, which saw nearly two dozen performances in 1869 alone, was joined in that year by the immediately popular *Hungarian Dances* (Books I and II) and *Liebeslieder* Waltzes, Op. 52, and together these works placed Brahms at the very forefront of German musical life – a circumstance that inevitably drew the ire of Richard Wagner.[2] From his eager publisher Fritz Simrock came repeated requests for new works, as in this letter of 16 March 1869: "I . . . can only repeat for the umpteenth time that I expect more soon: the [string] quartets and the symphony; come out with them finally – I'll give you no peace!"[3] Brahms ignored all these entreaties, but when in February 1870 Simrock offered a "lifetime contract," the composer responded in no uncertain terms (while alluding to the Classical tradition that weighed especially heavily upon his shoulders):

Stop pressuring your composers; it might become as dangerous as it generally is useless. One cannot compose one day like one might spin or sew. Some esteemed colleagues (Bach, Mozart, Schubert) have spoiled the world terribly. But if we can't imitate them in writing beautifully, we must certainly avoid wanting to [imitate them] in writing rapidly. It would also be unjust for you to put all the blame on idleness. Various things join together in making writing harder for us (my contemporaries), and many things for me especially. If only one would use us poets for some other purpose, you should see that we are of thoroughly and obviously industriousness natures. But I shall soon be able to give up looking for a "position"! A contract with you "for life"! But in that case the advantage would most probably be on my side. Anyway, I should be the one who could enter into it without hesitation – and therefore I prefer not do it![4]

Brahms hesitated, too, in the search to which he alluded here for a suitable professional post (or "secured position," as he described his goal in a remarkably similar letter that was written at the same time to his other primary publisher, J. Melchior Rieter-Biedermann). Although in 1869 and 1870 the composer contemplated pursuing positions in Cologne, Bonn, Berlin, Basel, Zürich, and even, as we have seen, provincial Sondershausen, he never took a serious step toward obtaining such a post, rightfully fearing the loss of his freedom in exchange for fixed and tedious duties.[5] Yet the prestigious directorship of the concerts of the Gesellschaft der Musikfreunde in Vienna, which came open in 1870 when Johann Herbeck resigned in order to become director of the Viennese Court Opera, was another matter, presenting rich artistic possibilities in the city that Brahms had finally come to call home. In the event, Brahms was offered leadership of the orchestra but not also, as he had insisted, of the choir, and on that account negotiations eventually ground to a halt. A triumphant performance of the *German Requiem* at the Gesellschaft concert of 5 March 1871 considerably enhanced Brahms's stock with the chorus membership, however, and by the spring of the following year he was able to accept an appointment on his own terms.[6]

Renewal of work and completion of the whole

Brahms's first program at the Gesellschaft was given on 10 November 1872. Included was Joachim's orchestration of Schubert's *Grand Duo* – or "Symphony in C major," as it was billed – about which Brahms wrote to his friend: "I don't have time to describe how beautiful you make everything sound, and what 'symphonic matters' ran through my head on this occasion."[7] But if the new music director's duties gave him valuable orchestral experience, it left him less time than before to tackle big compositional projects, and instead he concentrated his efforts on completing three significant works that had been lying unfinished for some years – the String Quartets in C Minor and A Minor, Op. 51 Nos. 1 and 2, and the Piano Quartet in C Minor, Op. 60. Yet by finally bringing these troubled pieces to completion and into print Brahms took some important steps along the path toward finishing his symphony. In the string quartets, he came to terms at last with the one other imposing genre in which he had long been inhibited by the example of Beethoven; in the piano quartet, as we shall see, he revisited the same difficult relationship with the Schumanns to which substantial reference is made in the first movement of the symphony. By the same token, the one major new work from this period – the *Variations on a Theme of Haydn*, conceived in the summer of 1873 as a work for two pianos (in which form it was published as Op. 56b) but soon transcribed for full orchestra (Op. 56a) – likewise brought Brahms closer to completing his symphony.

This remarkable story begins in May 1873, when Philipp Spitta presented the composer with the newly published first volume of his biography of J. S. Bach. That summer Brahms reciprocated the honor by sending Spitta an autograph of the organ fugue on "O Traurigkeit, o Herzeleid," WoO 7, at which time, stimulated by Spitta's account, he not only made certain inquiries of the author regarding Baroque ostinato technique, but, in the finale of the *Haydn Variations*, created his own magnificent set of ostinato variations, consisting of seventeen repetitions of a five-measure ground bass that was fashioned from the theme. At the end of the year Brahms presented Spitta with the autograph of the original piano duo version of this piece, and out of his enthusiasm for its finale Spitta arranged to have copies made for Brahms of several unpublished ostinato works by Buxtehude and Bach, including the latter's cantata "Nach dir, Herr, verlanget mich," BWV 150, copied on account of its closing chorus, which unfolds as a chaconne. Before long Spitta had come to know the recently published orchestral version of Brahms's variations, and when, on 9 February 1874, he dispatched the copies he added the following words of appreciation: "After this literally incomparable achievement in the realm of orchestral music the long cherished wish of all your admirers for a symphony will only be stirred up all the more."[8]

Although in the past Brahms had turned a deaf ear to the encouragement of his friends, this time he seems to have responded: serious work on the complex finale – stimulated, as I shall argue in Chapter 5, by a careful study of certain ostinato works by Bach – apparently was first begun in the ensuing summer, during the composer's sojourn in Rüschlikon, Switzerland.[9] Unfortunately, it is impossible to determine how far Brahms might have proceeded on the finale at this early stage; all material traces of his effort subsequently were destroyed. In any event, much work remained to be done when Brahms returned to Vienna in the fall of 1874 to begin his last season as director of the Gesellschaft concerts – in November he made it clear to Simrock that the symphony was not finished – and in the following summer, passed in Ziegelhausen bei Heidelberg, he quipped to his friend Franz Wüllner, music director in Munich, that he had chosen to work on a variety of "highly useless things" (including the String Quartet in B♭, Op. 67) in order to avoid having "to look a symphony straight in the face."[10] By the next year, however, Brahms was hard at work again on the piece. Perhaps he was stimulated by the impending Bayreuth première of that other long-awaited *magnum opus*, Wagner's *Ring* cycle; in any event, during a summer holiday spent in 1876 at remote Saßnitz, a Baltic Sea resort on the isle of Rügen, the last movement was finally completed.

To George Henschel, who joined the composer for ten days at Saßnitz, Brahms reflected on his creative process, in words that were prompted by an examination of Henschel's song "Wo Engel hausen," Op. 34 No. 3, but which speak tellingly about his own long experience with the symphony:

One ought never to forget that by actually perfecting *one* piece one gains and learns more than by commencing or half-finishing a dozen. Let it rest, let it rest, and keep going back to it and working at it over and over again, until it is completed as a finished work of art, until there is not a note too much or too little, not a measure you could improve upon. Whether it is *beautiful* also, is an entirely different matter, but perfect it *must* be. You see, I am rather lazy, but I never cool down over a work, once begun, until it is perfected, unassailable.[11]

At last the end was in sight. With the turbulent opening Allegro in C minor joined in place now by a victorious (purely instrumental) finale in C major – with the outlines of the plot-archetype of Beethoven's Fifth Symphony thereby firmly established – the suitable character and dimensions of the two middle movements could be envisioned. Brahms, working by turns in Hamburg and Lichtental, quickly completed a lyrical Poco Adagio in E and, in place of a true scherzo, an intermezzo-like Allegretto grazioso in A♭. The inscription appearing at the end of the autograph scarcely conveys all the sweat that went into the making of the whole; it reads simply: "J. Brahms Lichtenthal Sept. 76" (Plate 2.1).[12]

Pre-publication performances

Clara Schumann was vacationing in nearby Baden and saw a lot of Brahms at this time, but she knew nothing about his work until 25 September, when the composer played her the outer movements on the piano; a similar performance of the entire symphony followed on 10 October. Clara responded in much the same manner in which Bruch had initially greeted the *German Requiem*. She was impressed by the "ingenious" craftsmanship that was so evidently displayed in the music but "let down, disheartened," as she wrote in her diary, by its lack of "melodic warmth."[13] In the event, Brahms too was dissatisfied and, remaining faithful to the dictum that he had expressed to Henschel, he immediately worked the middle movements over some more.

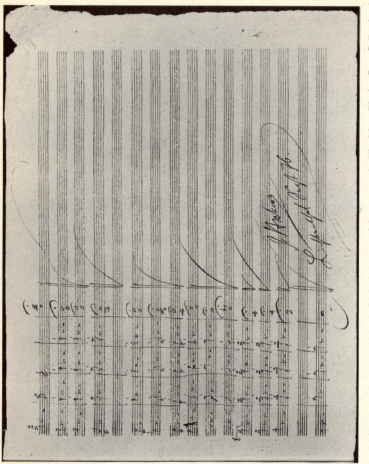
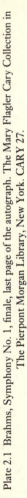

Plate 2.1 Brahms, Symphony No. 1, finale, last page of the autograph. The Mary Flagler Cary Collection in The Pierpont Morgan Library, New York. CARY 27.

What is unusual about this circumstance is not Brahms's decision to revise, but rather – after all the years of cautious work – the small amount of time that he left for this final stage before the première, which he scheduled for the first subscription concert of the Grand Ducal Court Orchestra in Karlsruhe on 4 November 1876. Privy to many details of this reworking was Otto Dessoff, the new Karlsruhe music director, whom Brahms greeted when he first arrived in neighboring Lichtental during the second week of September. Some mention apparently was made of the symphony at this meeting, but when Dessoff, who had already arranged to have a piano delivered to Brahms's quarters to facilitate his working, then eagerly placed his orchestra at his friend's disposal and even offered to see to the copying of parts, Brahms declined to take the bait. At the same time, rumors began to circulate that the work would be ready for the forthcoming season, and the composer soon received a large number of inquiries, not only from Simrock and Joachim in Berlin, but also, as we shall see, from several music directors who were angling for the first performance.[14]

Brahms's own preference, however, had always been to have the piece introduced by Dessoff in the relative obscurity of Karlsruhe. On the night of 11 October, having already decided to undertake a significant revision of the middle movements, he nevertheless wrote to Dessoff once more, explaining that he would like now to take advantage of his friend's offer to make the orchestral parts and then coyly adding: "Wouldn't the piece do for [your concert on] 4 November? (That isn't to importune, though.) But I know of nothing better for the opening jest [den ersten Spaß]."[15] Brahms was even more coy on the following day, when, as promised in his previous letter, the parts of the first movement and full score of the finale were sent off:

I don't know what I wrote to you yesterday in my drowsiness, since I returned home tired to find letters from Mannheim, Munich, and Vienna. It was my precious secret idea all along, of course, to hear the thing first in the small city that has a good friend, a good conductor, and a good orchestra. But since you never said a word, and the thing does not recommend itself on account of its charm – I ask therefore that the copying be taken care of with the speed of a brown bug [Mokkakäfer].[16]

At about the same time, Brahms responded to the invitations of Ernst Frank, conductor in Mannheim (who, on 14 October, replied in turn: "That is really magnificent! A symphony! That pleases me, not only for myself, but for all Germans!"); Franz Wüllner in Munich (who received the hasty note "Write and tell me the dates of your concerts in November. I'll be rehearsing a symphony very soon and can try it out with you on the return [to

Vienna]"); and Johann Herbeck, who in 1875 had succeeded Brahms as concert director of the Gesellschaft der Musikfreunde:

Please excuse my slowness, which I regret all the more since I was out the whole day and did not see until midnight the telegram you sent yesterday. Actually, I cannot write anything more than I cabled. It is possible that I will have a symphony performed this winter, but I do not want to read about it on the posters, and I therefore beg your discretion with regard to the following. I unfortunately cannot do more than promise you that I shall write something definite about the symphony in question as soon as possible. Then, however, I would like (for various reasons) to have a performance at one of the concerts early in the season. Could you let me know the dates? Orchestral works really belong to the Philharmonic; on the other hand there is my feeling of allegiance to your (our) fine institution, to which has now been added your kind invitation. For the time being, my thanks for your interest, and I am curious to know who has been having such a good look for you around my room and on my desk.[17]

Performances in Mannheim and Munich were quickly arranged (for 7 November and 15 November, respectively), and in a second letter to Herbeck a date was fixed for the all-important Viennese première: "There-fore we'll risk it on 17 December, even if I still have not heard the thing. That should take place, I think, on 4 November in Karlsruhe. (For a true first performance the more modest circumstances are certainly more agree-able to me.)"[18]

Brahms had more on his mind than arranging for performances of the new work, however; throughout this period, as we read in a letter of 17 October to his friend Theodor Billroth, he was struggling with the decision of whether to accept an offer to assume Schumann's old position as Municipal Music Director in Düsseldorf:

By now you will have learned through Faber that a call to Düsseldorf was bestowed upon me. I had hoped for a position, an activity, for so long and so earnestly, that I must now put on a serious expression to consider it. I am loath to leave Vienna and have all kinds of objections against Düsseldorf in particular. The question of money is also involved and Stockhausen's and Frau Schumann's appointments at the Con-servatory foundered on it (and little else). The attitude of the Ministry of Culture is, for the time being, very friendly, etc. In case of a Yes I would have to go there by New Year.

There is a bright side to everything, you will perhaps be saying now. For it is what brought me to the decision to come out with a symphony. I felt that I really ought to say good-bye to the Viennese by playing something worthwhile for them. Herbeck asked me for it (I have no idea how one had occurred to him), and I find it actually quite agreeable to be able to play it to the Gesellschaft and my choristers – even as I muse somewhat wistfully about the members of the Philharmonic.

Since a symphony by me is something of a rarity, it has already been telegraphed and written about profusely. I'll probably do it in Karlsruhe on the 4th of November, on the 9th [sic] in Mannheim, on the 15th in Munich, on the 17th of December in your vicinity.[19]

Brahms's wistful thinking about a performance of the new symphony in one of the concerts of the Vienna Philharmonic was in fact something of a ruse. Indeed, the composer's correspondence with Josef Hellmesberger, a leading figure at the Gesellschaft, suggests that the idea of programming the piece there instead had probably been planted in Herbeck's mind by none other than Brahms himself. On 2 October 1876, evidently in response to word that he had recently received from the composer, Hellmesberger replied: "The offering of your symphony for a Gesellschaft concert has absolutely delighted me, and I can hardly wait for this musical feast."[20] Brahms must have expected Hellmesberger, who had thus been given a "look around [Brahms's] room and on [his] desk," to bring the piece to Herbeck's attention with the hope of planning an early performance, and at least one of his "various reasons" seems clear: if Brahms really were to quit Vienna at the end of the year, then it is understandable that he would want to take his leave from the familiar podium of "his" Gesellschaft.[21]

Meanwhile, on 13 October, Dessoff acknowledged that he had received the manuscripts of the outer movements and dispatched them to the copyists. Then he continued:

You are a *Jesuwiter*! The parts for the first movement were written in Vienna (could have been duplicated a long time ago!) and now you come along and say that I never said a word concerning a performance here! O, you hypocrite! You know perfectly well that on the very day of your arrival I asked if you had something to rehearse – and if I didn't press you later on to have the piece performed here first, you know very well also that only timidity kept me from prevailing upon you to fulfill a request which you might have found annoying. I believe Kleinmichel would have been more forthcoming than you! And he wouldn't have had the movements come out begging separately, but rather have had [all four movements of] the whole symphony – lively, gentle, cheerful, and free [*die ganze Sinfonie frisch, fromm, fröhlich und frei*] – performed together in one place. He has the better of you there. – Yet it is lovely of you to want to try it out again with us. The musicians are delighted and send their best thanks in anticipation. And now come over here right away. Since falling barometric pressure is spreading over the entire continent, I hope you'll soon be brought down from Baden to Karlsruhe.[22]

Before he had received this letter, Brahms had already dashed off a brief note in which he promised to send the rest of the symphony on the following day: "Do say a word about the movements. I've made it short and easy for the copyist (and me?). But, hopefully, it won't be noticed that a drastic shortening has been made [*nur gewaltsam gekürzt ist*]. The finale demanded this consideration." The revised pieces then were shipped in due course on 14 October, at which time Brahms also included a two-measure insertion for the finale (mm. 417–18).[23]

Dessoff's reply is dated 16 October:

The two middle movements arrived in order and will be given to the copyist right away. The Adagio (although I was surprised at first by the initial four measures, which might be by someone other than Brahms) I find extraordinarily beautiful, indeed, ever more beautiful the more often I read it, which is always a good sign. If you really have shortened the piece, surely no one will take notice, so round and complete it is in form. As for the Intermezzo, I might well have wished that you hadn't shortened the ending so very much; the piece is so terse anyhow that the reason for this excessive laconicism isn't clear to me. Moreover, I find (in all humility and modesty!) the A♭ section much prettier than the Trio, and it is all the more sad for me that at the end one gets to hear so little more of it. Unless you have some very important reasons, think it over again, at least for publication.[24]

The conductor's wishes prevailed, and a few days later he received still another parcel from Brahms: "While sending herewith the desired first movement, I can't refrain from enclosing a supplement (in 3 NBs) for the Intermezzo. You might like to inscribe the two small NBs in the score – as for the larger one (18 [*recte:* 19] measures), show the copyist the right place! None of the ever-so-valuable measures from before has been omitted!!! I have in mind to send tomorrow a volume of supplements for all 4 movements!"[25]

These changes evidently are detectable in the autograph. The two entries made by Dessoff might be seen in measure 49, which shows a late addition of the first flute to continue its established doubling of the melodic line in the first oboe, and measures 111–12, which show an alteration whereby the original note values of a descending tetrachord were doubled and the single measure of the first layer was thus expanded into two. This augmentation, which, as we shall discover, helps clarify certain motivic relationships in the piece, was probably a new thought. In contrast, the large insertion (mm. 125–43), which Brahms set down on a different paper-type from that which he used in the rest of the score (fourteen staves instead of sixteen), most likely represents a simple restoration of some of the material that had originally been cut out of "consideration" for the finale. Yet even this restoration was not enough for Clara Schumann. Reflecting on her experience of the piece in the Leipzig performance of 18 January 1877, she complained: "The ending in the third movement was not completely satisfying to me, altogether too short." Brahms added nothing further, however, and, apart from a change in tempo from the original *Allegretto grazioso* to *Un poco Allegretto e grazioso*, the movement was published in same form in which it had been heard in the Karlsruhe première.[26]

The last-minute alterations made in the second movement were even more dramatic; these too ultimately were reconsidered, but not until the spring of 1877, when, to Simrock's joy, Brahms finally went about preparing the work for publication. Nearly fifty years ago, the British musicologist Sidney Newman inferred from the program notes that had been written for the performances in Cambridge (7 March 1877) and London (31 March and 16 April 1877) that this discarded version had been in an ABA'CA" rondo form, not the ternary form in which we know the work today. More recently, prompted by the discovery of some manuscript string parts that were used in the first performances, Robert Pascall and Frithjof Haas have offered reconstructions of what has been termed the "initial performing version."[27]

But how did this initial performing version compare with the original version that Brahms had played for Clara Schumann on 10 October 1876? Clara herself provides a hint in a letter 12 February 1877: "In one thing you have without knowing it come close to my wishes, with the alteration of the Adagio [*mit der Umänderung des Adagio*]. Between the first and last movements the spirit is, I feel, in need of some rest, of a song, at least at the beginning without the artful dress that obscures the awareness of the true melody."[28] This remark, with its implication that the beautiful song-like melody that is played by the oboe in measure 5 of the initial performing version had originally been introduced later, led Newman to surmise that the original version must have been largely identical to that of the first edition, wherein the oboe melody appears at measure 17. Disregarding Clara's testimony, Margit L. McCorkle has argued that it was not the published text but the initial performing version (what she calls the "penultimate version") that was identical with the version that Clara had heard in October 1876. Raymond Knapp, by contrast, has speculated that all three states were dissimilar from one another, with the first completed text (what he calls the

"Clara" version) being a full sonata form of considerably greater length than either of the two later ones.[29]

A rare preserved sketch for the movement, which evidently dates from mid-October 1876 and was uncovered on the obverse side of one of two leaves that were used as paste-overs in the autograph of the String Quartet in B♭, Op. 67, seems to confirm Newman's surmise (Plate 2.2).[30] To be sure, the sketch is closely related to the initial performing version; its first five systems contain the thematic substance of the A, B, and A′ sections of that distinctive text, which included some passages that are not found in the published version, as well as variant readings of others. But this does not imply that the original and initial performing versions were identical. For one thing, the sketch shows also a crucial idea, easily visible beneath Brahms's cancellation marks, that was withheld from the initial performing version but restored in the final text: the notable chromatic lines of measures 5–8, which stand out as a reference to the chromatic motto of the opening Allegro (mm. 38–42).

Herein lies the first clue that in writing the sketch Brahms in fact copied from a well-developed draft that already showed both the thematic outline and ternary form of the published text. A second clue can be read into the breaking-off point of Brahms's notation in the middle of the fifth system, at the beginning of what in the rondo form of the initial performing version is the second episode. According to the scenario being proposed here Brahms would have had no need to proceed further in the sketch, since the C section of the rondo duplicates the middle sections of the published version, and the last return of the rondo theme-group offers little more than a simple reorchestration of the opening.[31]

The same assumption helps to explain also the exceptional appearance of the sketch. Though Brahms entered his notations onto several systems of piano score, he seldom used more than the treble clef. There was, of course, no need in most instances to "compose" but merely to arrange a new sequence of material already in existence. Thus the sketch may be seen as a kind of line score, with a virtually continuous melody and only an occasional accompanying or contrapuntal voice, most notably at the beginning of the newly created first episode (B), an inversion canon based upon the head motif of the main theme. It served, in other words, as an aid in transforming one "finished" version of the movement into another, very different one. And in light of the succession of ideas in the sketch, we must dismiss Knapp's position that the original "finished" version had been a comparatively lengthy sonata form and can only conclude that the first and final versions must have been very much alike.[32]

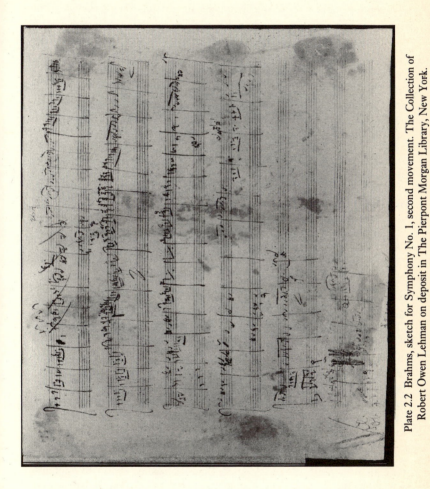

Plate 2.2 Brahms, sketch for Symphony No. 1, second movement. The Collection of Robert Owen Lehman on deposit in The Pierpont Morgan Library, New York.

Later revisions and publication

Simrock attended the première and left Karlsruhe hoping that he might be given the music after the Viennese performance in December and so be able to announce publication of the symphony for the following February. But Brahms had in mind to schedule some additional trial performances and would do no more than promise that "in the event I really like the thing finally, I think we'll occupy the engravers with it during the summer holidays!!"[33] The publisher had little choice except to bide his time quietly, but when in early April 1877 he learned that Joachim, who had conducted the piece in Cambridge, had returned from England without the score (which was still needed there for the London performance on 16 April), he began to show the composer his anxiety, as in this letter of 12 April:

For every possible and impossible reason I find it truly imprudent simply to give up the manuscript to strange hands!! Hopefully everything will soon be in your hands; I'd like it out by the beginning of September and repeat that it is not always easy to have good engravers at just any time. Could I at least count on it by the beginning of June? Nevertheless, if you do really intend to make more changes, then could you estimate how much time – *at the outside* – will be needed for that?

Then there was still to be addressed the matter of the honorarium, which for such a watershed work would have to be considerably higher than usual. Simrock continued almost sheepishly:

Nothing seems more awkward at this time, for me – [than] to make you an offer! I confess – I shouldn't really know how to go about doing it, and it'll certainly be better if you leave matters as they were and make a demand in line with *your* opinion: – for besides, this would be the critical one and nothing could be more distressing to *me* than to have a misunderstanding with you in such matters! Just believe me, as I told you at the beginning of our relation – and I can only go on repeating it – that your demand is never too high for me. For that reason, I think, you thus might like to continue the practice followed up to now – and for the rest not grieve me by handing your manuscripts over to other publishers – be it only songs or anything else – I am *personally* devoted to every note of yours.[34]

In his next letter, dated 25 April, Simrock readily agreed to Brahms's request for the princely sum of 5000 Talers (15,000 Marks), and then went on some more with his worries about the score: "But the matter with the roast beefs [i.e., the English] is a distress – the symphony was given on the 16th and then should have been sent off straightaway; I'm afraid it's being sent as a parcel, which requires fourteen days more, which is like an *eternity*;

registered printed matter, well tied, is simplest and as fast as a letter, – in that case you'd have had it long ago already."[35] In the event, the music arrived back safely in Vienna at the beginning of May, and Brahms was able to devote the remainder of that month to the task of making the symphony ready for the press. The complete score and parts for all but the newly cast Andante were in Simrock's possession by the beginning of June. The symphony was to become Brahms's Op. 68. Even on its title page it would stake its claim for a place next to the *Ur*-Symphony in C minor: Beethoven's Fifth, Op. 67.[36]

In June, in the midst of preparing the four-hand piano arrangement, Brahms had some second thoughts about the tempo of the finale; it had been played *Allegro con brio* during the trial performances and then been inscribed *Allegro moderato ma con brio* in the engraver's model, but only now was it given its definitive marking of *Allegro non troppo ma con brio*. Some weeks later Brahms sent along a new five-measure replacement for the final three measures of the slow movement. And at the end of the busy summer – during which Brahms found time to compose nearly the whole of his Second Symphony – he requested that the strings be marked *largamente* in the counterstatement of the finale's main subject (mm. 186ff.). All these changes were incorporated into the final text, and in early October Simrock was able at long last to announce the work, which appeared a few weeks later in both full score and the composer's four-hand piano arrangement.[37]

On 31 October Simrock sent Brahms a beautifully bound copy of the new score:

I'd like to have found a binding that corresponds better to the magnificence of the contents, but then it might easily have seemed as though the binding wished to claim importance alongside the contents: so take the will for the well-meaning deed! The volume seems durable at least; but even the most durable one will have long since turned to dust when spirit and soul of all those whose feelings are devoted to the noble and beautiful in our art are still being rejuvenated and lifted by the contents.[38]

Brahms was greatly moved by the present and truly grateful for the sentiment:

I don't know whether you have enough imagination to conceive how happy I'm made by your kindness and how thankful I am to you! To describe that isn't easy of course – the emotion is hard to describe in words! Indeed, imagine in all earnestness how a composer is overjoyed, and since you know me well enough to know that I am not exactly vain, then you know that as for all the luxury I truly enjoy only your great kindness! The ... sumptuous volume ... lies on the piano and delights and amazes everyone – I must keep young composers from looking at it, otherwise too many symphonies would come to you! ... And now emotion is seizing me again, and I'll go and feast my eyes and whisper to you my thanks![39]

When we remember the years of struggle that went into the making of the symphony, these heartfelt words seem all the more meaningful.

Structure and meaning in the first movement

One doesn't quite know where the enormous virtuosity of workmanship stops and the music begins.[1]

Only music could free the young man, maturing to manhood through suffering, from the heavy burden of his experiences; Werther–Manfred conjured up Astarte and drafted the Allegro of the C Minor Symphony. This first movement bears the sign of Manfred unmistakably on its forehead.[2]

I

The slow introduction to the First Symphony (Un poco sostenuto) was a memorable afterthought. Although we know that when Albert Dietrich and Clara Schumann laid eyes on the score in the summer of 1862 the music began straightaway with the opening Allegro's four-measure chromatic motto (mm. 38–42), we unfortunately possess no similar first-hand evidence of when Brahms might later have supplied the dark new beginning. Raymond Knapp has speculated that the critical addition came only toward the end of the symphony's long gestation period, being but one step in a thoroughgoing process of late revision in which all four movements were refitted to one degree or another. In this view, Brahms was concerned above all with balancing the weight of the two outer movements, the two poles in the symphony's dramatic narrative of *per aspera ad astra*. On the one hand, Knapp speculates, this seems to have involved making a significant cut in a grand finale that threatened otherwise to overwhelm the first movement, with its brisk $\frac{6}{8}$ rhythm and scherzo-like character; on the other, it also meant creating for that first movement a dramatic slow introduction, without which it might not hold its own as a worthy "dark" foil to the powerful "light" that shines forth from the imposing finale.[3]

At all events – and we shall have occasion in Chapter 5 to consider the unusual structure of the finale that led Knapp to this supposition – the introduction at once establishes the fateful tragic tone of the movement and foreshadows much of its thematic material. The loud opening phrase is derived fairly directly from the abrupt motto-like beginning of the Allegro, likewise beginning with the notes C–C♯–D set off against a descending chromatic line in parallel thirds (compare mm. 1ff. and 38ff.). What is new in the introduction is an ominous tonic pedal point in the timpani, contra-bassoon, and double basses, which leaves no mistaking the work's serious purpose. After building to a tremendous half cadence on the notes F–F♯–G (by means of an augmented-sixth chord, a predictable outcome of the chromatic voice leading and, like the chromatic motto, one of the symphony's most characteristic sounds), the music continues with a quiet, tense passage that will recur shortly as the tempestuous continuation of the movement's main theme (compare mm. 9ff. and 51ff.). A pair of open diminished sevenths, whose starkness here is enhanced by the pizzicato strings, alternates with close four-part harmony that struggles with the chromatic language as if mired in some thick substance.

Breaking free at last over an extended Neapolitan-sixth chord (another characteristic sound), flute, bassoon, and first violins unfold a long scalewise descent that leads to a second pedal point, now on the dominant, under-girding an adumbration of the main theme itself (compare mm. 21ff. and 42ff.). Beginning as a slow and quiet arpeggiation of the notes G and E♭, this passage quickly blazes up into an abbreviated climactic return, on the same dominant pedal, of the opening material. Only now does Brahms introduce the first real tune in the movement, a plaintive melody for the solo oboe (the first of the symphony's many important melodies for this instrument); the flute initiates a counterstatement but that soon breaks down, and in the end the cellos are left to carry the melancholy tune in a second scalewise descent to a quiet, expectant half close in their lowest register.

The stormy Allegro that breaks out suddenly at measure 38 is, of all the movements in the symphony, the one that is most indebted to Beethoven, whose famous "C minor mood" is reflected in both the intense rhythmic drive that Brahms sustains throughout much of the music, as well as his dramatic handling of the main turning points in the form. The motto itself, as Michael Musgrave has noted, shows certain similarities to the flourish that opens the Allegro of the *Les adieux* Sonata, Op. 81a, while the tonal plan of the ensuing exposition – with the progression i–III–iii, leading to VII at the start of the development – recalls that of the *Appassionata* Sonata, Op. 57.[4] But surely the most telling links are made to the Fifth Symphony, the very work in which Brahms's chosen plot-archetype originated. The coupling of the key of C minor with the iconic "fate rhythm" (♩♩♩|♩.) are only the most obvious points of contact between the two works; a more subtle resonance comes at the end of Brahms's recapitulation (mm. 462ff.), where the expected final cadence is undercut and the vehement closing gesture made to spill over into a coda that acts as a second development (cf. mm. 370ff. in Beethoven's Fifth).

Although these broad allusions to the Fifth Symphony are unmistakable – and were surely intended to be heard as such – the opening Allegro is thoroughly characteristic of Brahms's own style.[5] The movement is one of the composer's most densely packed creations, rightly celebrated as a *locus classicus* of his mastery of motivic counterpoint and concern for "thematic unity" (see Table 3.1). In keeping with its scherzo idiom, the momentum is unflagging; one passage flows restlessly into the next, each forming a tributary to a churning stream of related ideas. Thus the chromatic motto forms an essential part of each of the exposition's three theme groups (in C minor, E♭ major, and E♭ minor). At the outset, as Giselher Schubert has recently noted, its upper line – three ascending chromatic half steps followed by a descending stepwise passage in dotted rhythm with sixteenth notes – serves as the first main idea of a "double theme" (mm. 38–42) whose impassioned second main idea (mm. 42ff.) – the primary theme *per se* (likewise consisting of complementary ascending and descending gestures) – it serves as counterpoint (Example 3.1a).[6] Beyond that, the exposition offers little in the way of genuine thematic differentiation. Instead, the two main elements of the double theme recur over and over, marking the counterstatement of the primary group (mm. 70ff.) and both the secondary and closing groups (mm. 121ff. and 157ff., respectively), appearing here in their original forms, there in inversion, and often in invertible counterpoint (Example 3.1b–d). Following a strong cadence in measure 185 (the first to appear in some 100 measures), the exposition concludes with a violent transformation of the main theme, now distilled to its opening pair of thirds, set in the minor mode, turned backwards, and hammered out several times in succession (Example 3.1e). The development and coda, in turn, each reveal still other transmogrifications. Table 3.1 recounts much of this story, but in the end it can scarcely do justice to Brahms's seemingly endless capacity for wringing every last bit of potential from his tiny motivic ideas.

Difficult, too, to capture in such a table is the fluidity of Brahms's form, which has already been remarked in regard to the merging of the recapitulation and coda. Consider the transition. Although the arrival on the tonic in the strings on the downbeat of measure 89 completes a perfect cadence and

Table 3.1

Measure	Description
1–38	*Slow introduction*

38–189a	*Exposition*

Group I in C minor + transition (mm. 38–121)

Chromatic motto (mm. 38–42), leading to (and serving as counterpoint in bass to) open-ended main theme (mm. 42–51), followed by continuation (mm. 51–70). Extended counterstatement, with motto inverted and Beethovenian "fate rhythm" added (mm. 70–89), elided to transition (mm. 89–121, consisting of many different phrases, with much emphasis on V/E♭ minor)

Group II in E♭ major (mm. 121–56)

Motto and main theme combined in invertible counterpoint (mm. 121–30), leading to lyrical second theme (mm. 130–8), whose cadential figure forms the basis for a lengthy continuation (with "purple patch"), dying away finally on E♭ minor (mm. 138–56)

Closing group in E♭ minor (mm. 157–89)

Introduced by *marcato* descending stepwise thirds in fate rhythm (mm. 157–60), leading to contrapuntal combination of this "fate motif" + chromatic motto with inverted main theme in double counterpoint (mm. 161–77), elided to "drive to cadence" combining fate motif with cadential idea from Group II (mm. 177–85) and final, hammered thirds based on part of transition (mm. 185–9)

189b–343	*Development*

Part I (mm. 189b–97): Loud canonic treatment of main theme in B major (similar in form to counterstatement), ending with half cadence

Part II (mm. 197–225): Quiet mysterious treatment of main theme, beginning in B major but drifting into C major. Suddenly interrupted by

Part III (mm. 225–73): Begins with fate motif in B♭ minor (over C triad), but itself soon interrupted by new, chorale theme in G♭ major, setting off a chain of modulations: G♭ major/F♯ minor–A major; A major/A minor–C major. Fate motif re-emerges and leads to half cadence in C minor on the motif F–F♯–G, repeated several times with decreasing dynamics and forming basis of

Part IV (mm. 273–93): Quiet dominant pedal supporting motto-derived material reminiscent of slow introduction, dying away inconclusively at the end on I_4^6 in B minor before being gradually brought back to life in

Part V (mm. 293–321): inexorable Beethovenian "swell" combining motto and smoothed-out fate theme, leading to

Part VI (mm. 321–43): climactic peak, contrapuntally combining end of *Schicksalsmotive* and fate theme over dominant pedal. Resolved deceptively into B minor by return of chromatic motto transposed to begin on F♯ and continuing sequentially back to V/V–V in C minor (as in the original form of the motto) and ultimate resolution to

343–462	*Recapitulation*

Group I in C minor + transition (mm. 343–94)

Begins directly with main theme. End of continuation, entire counterstatement, and beginning of transition cut and replaced by short new link: thus mm. 343–69 (= mm. 42–68) + mm. 370–1 (new) + mm. 372–94 (= mm. 99–121 transposed down by minor third).

Group II in C major (mm. 394–429)
(= mm. 121–56, transposed)

Closing group in C minor (mm. 430–)
(= mm. 157–89 transposed), elided to

462–511	*Coda*

so evidently closes off the preceding counterstatement of the main theme, it is actually the preceding dominant chord that sets the ensuing modulation going, initiating a quasi-sequential passage (with dovetailed echoes in the woodwinds) that eventually leads to $V^9/E\flat$ minor at measure 97. Nor is the beginning of the second group, whenever it comes, a clear-cut matter. Does it really start at measure 121, when a new combination of the two elements of the double theme greet the major mediant key, emerging in attenuated fashion by means of the progression V^2–I^6? Does the fleeting appearance of a partly new lyrical melody in the oboe at measure 130 constitute a more significant event? Or, as Raymond Knapp has understood the reading that is offered in one recent recording, does the real point of arrival not come until much later, with the beautiful dialogue between clarinet and horn beginning in measure 148?[7]

Even more striking are the ambiguities surrounding the motto itself. What kind of gesture is it? Does it really form the first part of a "double theme"? Although its unusual harmonic progression – three chromatic chords (culminating in an augmented sixth) yielding to tonal clarification (V/V–V–i) – betrays its origins as an introductory gesture, it is, after all, included in the repetition of the exposition and so must be understood as forming an integral part of the first group. Yet when the motto makes its dramatic return at measure 335, following a lengthy dominant pedal point that seems to foretell the imminent beginning of the recapitulation, it scarcely forms the expected

Example 3.1: (a) I, 38–46; (b) I, 70–2; (c) I, 121–3; (d) I, 161–5; (e) I, 185–8

structural downbeat. Instead it constitutes a temporary tonal retreat, and only after reproducing itself as so many links in a chromatic chain (cf. mm. 121ff.), does the motto lead back to a decisive return of the main theme itself, and with that to the unequivocal beginning of the recapitulation.

If Brahms's display of compositional technique is impressive, it was bound to leave some listeners, even sympathetic ones, cold. The music is "not exactly charming," as the composer himself acknowledged, echoing in his own ironic manner Clara Schumann's opinion that all the "ingenious" craftsmanship had come at the expense of genuine "melodic warmth." And though Clara later judged the symphony to be "wonderful, grand, completely overpowering," she none the less remained dissatisfied by the second theme [*zweite Motiv*], which was "not rich enough" and lacked "élan."[8]

Speaking in the same vein to Ernst Rudorff, a colleague of hers in the 1870s at the Berlin Hochschule (where Joachim programmed the work in November 1877), Clara confessed that she had "found little outstanding about the ideas of the first part of the Allegro; only with the so-called development in the second part was the music thrilling and significant."[9] Clara's reaction to the exposition, given its relentless chromaticism and dissonant harmonies, accords well with her known preference for a more lyrical style; even Brahms's "zweite Motiv" evidently failed to embody this in a degree sufficient enough to suit her taste. But the development was in her opinion a different matter − and one can only agree that it is indeed thrilling and significant.

The loud and agitated manner of the closing group, in nearly every measure of which sounds the ominous fate rhythm, is at first continued across the double bar, as the Gb and Eb from the final measures of the exposition are respelled enharmonically as F♯ and D♯ and turned backwards to initiate a broad canonic treatment of the main theme in B major (mm. 189–97). This tumultuous bridge then gives way to a series of several larger paragraphs, beginning with a hushed and mysterious passage (mm. 192–225) in which the main theme drifts surprisingly into the key of C major (the tonal goal of the symphony).

That moment of calm is soon shattered, however. The head motif of the closing theme (on the notes Db–C–Bb) returns with a start at measure 225, first transforming the quiet C major triad into a sinister ninth chord, and then, just as unexpectedly, leading to a new chorale-like melody in the distant key of Gb major (mm. 233ff.). Kalbeck heard in this theme − surely Clara found much to admire in its beautiful, sonorous qualities − an allusion to the final phrase of the chorale "Ermuntre dich"; others have noted a similarity between the theme and the chorale-like phrase that links the final two movements of Beethoven's "Pastoral" Symphony (Example 3.2).[10] At all events, the music again begins to modulate to C major, and this time there is no "drifting" about it; on the contrary, the theme, fully scored and played *fortissimo*, unfolds the most direct kind of tonal relations along its tonal swerve: Gb major–F♯ minor–A major; A major–A minor–C major (mm. 240–52). But once more the head motif of the closing theme disrupts matters, gradually supplanting the chorale and then leading immediately to a fierce

Example 3.2: (a) Brahms, First Symphony, I, 232–6; (b) "Ermuntre dich" (last phrase); (c) Beethoven, Sixth Symphony, IV, 146–50

half cadence in C *minor*, repeated several times and gradually petering out in the lower strings and bassoons.

The ensuing paragraph (mm. 273–93) grows directly out of that half cadence (F–F♯–G) but also looks back even further in the movement to the slow introduction, which it recalls through its combination of ascending motto, descending chromatic thirds, and pedal point (here on V). Seemingly poised to become the retransition, the passage instead sinks slowly under its own weight, and when finally even the firm bass is pushed down by a half step, to F♯, all motion ceases on a I$^6_4$ chord in B minor. From this moment of deathly stillness – and tonal remove – comes one of the most visceral passages in all of Brahms (mm. 293–321). Setting out quietly with the motto in the contrabassoon and basses on the same low F♯, the music gradually builds in momentum through a long climb into an ever-expanding register. The upper strings (with bowed tremolo in the violas and second violins) enter in free imitation and join the basses in transforming the motto by "stretching" its last interval yearningly upward. Meanwhile the timpani and horns contribute the ominous fate rhythm; the upper woodwinds, the related head motif of the closing theme (doubled in thirds and made legato). When, in measures 318–21, the first violins offer one final run-through of the crucial notes F♯–G–A♭ (embodying both the motto and the "stretched" intervals at one fell swoop), they carry the music over the summit and unleash, on an excruciating V^9 chord, a violent rushing descent that – after one last detour at measure 335 – leads at last to the recapitulation (mm. 343ff.).

The dominant pedal point and fate rhythm are restored with a vengeance in this climactic tutti, and the familiar head motif of the closing theme holds the place in the texture that it had won in the preceding blaze-up. But at the

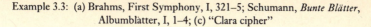

Example 3.3: (a) Brahms, First Symphony, I, 321–5; Schumann, *Bunte Blätter*,
Albumblätter, I, 1–4; (c) "Clara cipher"

outset of the passage the ascending three-note chromatic motto momentarily yields to its complement, the descending stepwise figure from measures 40–2, which is repeated several times in a driving circle-of-fifths progression. (Example 3.3a.) Although this idea had often percolated underneath the surface, it is only here, at the climax of the development, that it emerges into real thematic prominence. Significantly, its shape is identical with the theme from the first *Albumblatt* in Robert Schumann's *Bunte Blätter*, Op. 99, which incorporates a musical encoding of his wife's name (Example 3.3b–c).[11] In 1854, Clara (Op. 20) and Brahms himself (Op. 9) each published a free-standing set of variations for piano on the same theme. Brahms's work, in particular, possesses an extraordinary "private" character, based in his deep and complex relationships with Robert and Clara, and something of the intimacy of the music may be gathered from the inscription that is found on the autograph: "Kleine Variationen über ein Tema von Ihm. Ihr zugeeignet" ("Little Variations on a Theme of His, Dedicated to Her"). The reappearance of this theme at the climax of Brahms's later symphonic movement, then, would seem to call for some reflection.[12]

II

As an ever-growing number of studies reminds us, Brahms was no paragon of absolute music, no musical autonomist – least of all in his early years. The "Schumann" Variations scarcely stand alone in this respect. We have noted already Joachim's report that the opening of the First Piano Concerto (drafted in 1854) represents a "visualization of Schumann's suicide attempt";

Example 3.4: Schumann, *Genoveva*, No. 4, 53–6

Mei - nes Wei - bes nimm dich an.

and to that evidence can be added Brahms's own description of this work's slow movement as "a gentle portrait" of Clara.[13] More remarkable still is the first version of the Piano Trio in B Major, Op. 8 (1854), whose numerous allusions – above all, to Schumann's opera *Genoveva* – stamp the work with "an unmistakable undertone of autobiographical fantasy."[14] Brahms could hardly have overlooked the parallels between the story of this opera and his own predicament of the moment: Golo, whose duty it is to watch protectively over Genoveva in the battle-time absence of her husband, Siegfried, instead falls hopelessly in love with her. Of particular interest is Schumann's setting of Siegfried's departing charge to Golo to "take care of my wife" ("Meines Weibes nimm dich an"). As Kalbeck noted, this B minor version of Schumann's "Clara cipher" later served Brahms as a basic thematic idea throughout his trio (Example 3.4).[15]

Striking, too, is the first movement of the Piano Quartet in C Minor, Op. 60, which was completed only in the earlier 1870s but whose first movement (in its original key of C♯ minor) Brahms shared with Clara in the spring of 1855: on several occasions in later years – in some of his frankest remarks about the poetic content of his own works – Brahms pointedly likened this music to the tale of Goethe's *Werther* (whose protagonist commits suicide out of his guilt for having loved the wife of an older, respected friend).[16] And when we recognize that Brahms began this quartet with an allusion to the beginning of Schumann's Fourth Symphony, with similar sustained octaves yielding to the familiar musical transliteration of Clara's name, we may assume that he knew very well that Schumann had originally intended the Fourth as a kind of "Clara Symphony" (Example 3.5).[17]

That assumption, in turn, affects our understanding of Brahms's symphonic Allegro. Although Kalbeck's conviction that this movement too reflected "the heavy burden of [Brahms's] experiences" with the Schumanns in the mid–1850s raises fewer skeptical eyebrows today than it once did, the fact remains that no documentary evidence of the work is to be found before 1862 (long after Robert's death and the conclusion of Johannes's dangerous liaison with Clara).[18] But we need not settle the question of dating in order to profit from Kalbeck's notion that the roots of the music somehow lay in the young composer's troubled personal life. And after all the evidence has been

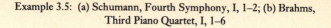

Example 3.5: (a) Schumann, Fourth Symphony, I, 1–2; (b) Brahms,
Third Piano Quartet, I, 1–6

sorted out, I hope to have shown that the first movement does indeed "bear the sign of Manfred on its forehead."

In keeping with his autobiographical interpretation, Kalbeck identified the primary theme as a picture of Brahms himself, delineated in an early instance of the composer's putative *Wahlspruch* "Frei aber froh" ("Free but happy") (see Example 3.1a).[19] We ought to proceed cautiously here, however. Brahms's theme sets out with a distinctive four-note motif (E♭–G–E♭–G), not with any of the three-note motifs that might logically be derived from the expression "Frei aber froh" (e.g., F–A–F, F–A♭–F, or F♯–A–F♯, in any transposition). Nor, for that matter, is there any solid evidence that such three-note patterns themselves, which indisputably form an important feature of the composer's stylistic idiom, ever carried any of the biographical significance that Kalbeck attributed to them.[20]

On the other hand, we might find a source for Brahms's primary theme – and justification for hearing in it a certain autobiographical resonance – in the primary theme of Schumann's Fourth Symphony (beginning D–F–D–F) (Example 3.6a). As Christopher Reynolds has argued, Brahms frequently paid tribute to Schumann just by means of echoing this pattern. In this case, however, Brahms recalls not only this "Schumann cipher" but also – and this likewise is found in Schumann's Fourth – the same "Clara cipher" that figures prominently in both Brahms's B Major Trio and *Werther* Quartet.[21]

41

Example 3.6: (a) Schumann, Fourth Symphony, I, 29; (b) Brahms, First Symphony, I, 42–6

But whereas Schumann, in his "Clara Symphony," had linked the two ideas in a kind of musical marriage, Brahms never allows them to be joined (Example 3.6b). On the contrary, in his opening Allegro it is not the "Schumann cipher" but the ominous chromatic motto (C–C#–D) that is bound into the music representing Clara – who then appears, significantly, in a form that recalls Schumann's setting, in *Genoveva*, of the admonition "Meines Weibes nimm dich an." Thus the emotional flavor of the movement, wherein both the motto and Clara cipher play significant roles, is enhanced by the recognition that the strenuous theme which seems a portrait of Brahms draws its lines from material that represents Schumann: in a phrase, Johannes as Robert.

But might not this theme also, as Kalbeck had it, represent Brahms as Manfred–Werther? At the very time when the first movement of the *Werther* Quartet was written the composer was immersed in study of Schumann's *Scenes from Faust* and *Manfred*. Brahms put it thus in a breathless letter to Clara of 21 March 1855:

If only I could have heard the *Manfred* music with you! That, with the *Faust*, is the most magnificent thing your husband [has] created. But I'd like to hear it as a whole and in combination with the text. What a deeply moving impression it must make. Often the melodramatic passages are incomprehensible to me, such as Astarte's appearance and speaking. That is the very highest form of musical delivery; that penetrates right into the depths of the heart.[22]

Now, in view of the powerful impression that *Manfred* so clearly had made on Brahms, it would not be surprising to find allusions to this composition in his own music of the time. Indeed, the subject of the Fugue in A♭ Minor for Organ, WoO 8, which Brahms wrote "ganz eigentlich für Clara" and presented to her in honor of Robert's birthday on 8 June 1856, virtually quotes the second theme of the *Manfred* Overture (Example 3.7). The

Example 3.7: (a) Brahms, Fugue in A♭ Minor, 1–3; (b) Schumann, *Manfred* Overture, 217–22

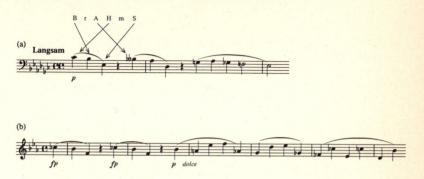

program of the latter piece, in turn, sheds light on Brahms's probable intention: since Schumann's second theme represents the beloved (sister) Astarte, Brahms's fugue subject might well refer to the beloved (married) Clara. Yet – and this will become important later – when Brahms sent a copy of this fugue for Adolf Schubring's inspection in July 1856, he implied, in remarks that raise once more the probability that the composer was engaged in a kind of dangerous "role playing," that he had encoded his own signature within the music, presumably referring to the first four notes of the subject, which can be derived from a musical transliteration of his name: B[=B♭]–r–A[=B♭♭]–H[=C♭]–m–S[=E♭].[23]

It is all the more remarkable, then, that the first movement of the C Minor Symphony rehearses much of this material, with its suggestive, intertwined references to "Johannes, Robert, and Clara" (Example 3.8). Once again the distinctive head motif of Schumann's second theme figures prominently, serving this time as the springboard for Brahms's own second theme, which then proceeds to weave the two heterophonically related voices of Schumann's chromatically descending subject into a single melodic line. Even the background textures of the two themes are similar. Both are set over smooth, slower moving chromatic harmonies fashioned out of voices moving in contrary motion.

Kalbeck, who staked a good deal on this reminiscence, was not the only member of Brahms's circle to take note of the allusion. It was recognized by Clara herself, as we learn from the same recollection of Ernst Rudorff that we had occasion to quote earlier:

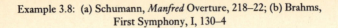

Example 3.8: (a) Schumann, *Manfred* Overture, 218–22; (b) Brahms,
First Symphony, I, 130–4

I remember from a conversation with Frau Schumann how she, for her part, evaluated the first movement. She found little outstanding about the ideas of the first part of the Allegro; only with the so-called development in the second part was the music thrilling and significant. Moreover, in the second subject she discovered a reminiscence of Schumann's *Manfred* Overture. She explained that when she expressed this to him one day, Brahms retorted with irritation: "Yes, I know, of course, that I have no individuality" ["Ja, ich weiss ja, dass ich keine Individualität habe."][24]

The "hermeneutic window" thus opened on the symphony invites us to look for additional relationships between the two works – and these are easy enough to find. Indeed, Brahms's opening Allegro, shot through with extreme tension, inhabits the same brooding and agitated atmosphere as Schumann's overture.[25] Both unfold comparable unusual tonal plans, involving the dark key of E♭ minor and a second group based on contrast between parallel modes, with Schumann's exposition modulating from E♭ minor to G♭ (F♯) minor to G♭ (F♯) major, and Brahms's passing from C minor to E♭ major to E♭ minor. Moreover, the grim, restless mood of each work is achieved through similar means: by using motivic themes instead of lyrical ones, by basing much on a pithy chromatic cell and employing frequent (and unsettling) changes in mode, by avoiding strong perfect cadences within sections and blurring the edges between them. And if Brahms does not quite match Schumann's complete avoidance of even a single full close within his exposition, he does maintain great tension by withholding until the very end of his rather longer first part (for more than 100 measures) any perfect cadence in the second key (major or minor), consistently employing, as Schumann had done, first-inversion harmony where a root-position tonic is expected and so undercutting any sense of stability and closure.[26]

Yet Brahms's "individuality" cannot be questioned, and his creative "misreading" of *Manfred* is thorough and (thoroughly) convincing.[27] Schumann's overture, for example, gets underway with an explosion of three rapid-fire, syncopated chords; this is "a provocative, violent, unstable motto," as James Webster has described it, "whose only weakness (if that is the right term) is that it is abandoned for the rest of the composition."[28] This motto yields immediately to a slow tempo and chromatic lines fanning outward in contrary motion; the ensuing passage includes several anticipations of the movement's main theme, but the motto, indeed, is not heard from again. By contrast, Brahms's first movement, in its initial form without slow introduction, begins by conflating the two ideas of Schumann's opening into a single bold and striking gesture (see Example 3.1a). Here the initial explosive chords themselves embody the wedge-like chromatic lines (what Kalbeck termed the *Schicksalsmotiv*) and then elide into a rushing stepwise passage – related to the Clara cipher – that leads to a strong cadence in the tonic (mm. 38–42). Moreover, far from abandoning this motto (as Schumann had done), Brahms allows hardly any subsequent idea to be left untouched by its chromatic voice leading.[29]

Although the musical logic displayed across the entire exposition allows for a coherent "absolute" understanding of the music, it might also be offered in support of Kalbeck's metaphorical reading of the movement. The paucity of thematic materials and the severity with which they are treated, the inability of the music ever to shake free of the motto's anxious chromatic grip – can we not hear in all this something of Manfred's struggle with oppressive guilt over his love for Astarte and so, by extension, Brahms's own internal wrestling on account of his "forbidden" relationship with Clara?

Ironically, the credibility of such an interpretation rides to a large degree on the one brief respite from all the struggling that emerges in the second theme – and with that, of course, we return to the matter of Brahms's allusion to the *Manfred* Overture. The gruff manner in which the composer forestalled any discussion of this question when it was raised by Clara Schumann is entirely in keeping with what we know from other anecdotes of his behavior upon having his allusions remarked on by others.[30] Yet, in view of the evidently sensitive personal nature of this example in particular, we might well read something more into Brahms's evasiveness. For the allusion to *Manfred* ran deeper than Kalbeck (or even Clara) seems to have suspected, involving not only the second theme of the overture but Schumann's melodramatic setting of Astarte's appearance and speaking (No. 10 in Schumann's score), the scene, that is, in which Manfred is finally released from his guilt, the very one, indeed, that Brahms had singled out for admiration in his letter to Clara of 21 March 1855.

The text of this crucial scene is given in Table 3.2, with Byron's original in the left-hand column, F. W. Suckow's German translation in the right-hand column, and three subdivisions (reflecting the main sections of Schumann's setting), indicated in the margins. Manfred at first makes do with minimal musical accompaniment, as he begins his impassioned address to the conjured spirit. Out of this, in a lengthy middle section, flows a beautiful "song with spoken words" during which the guilt-ridden Manfred renews again and again his entreaty to the silent spirit for forgiveness and mercy. In the end, Astarte is moved to grant her pardoning word.

Of particular interest is the music that underlies Astarte's final line of verse. Prominent here is a recollection by the woodwinds of the first two measures of the overture's "Astarte" theme – of the melody, that is, which both Clara and Kalbeck thought to be the source of Brahms's own second theme (see the top line in Example 3.9a). But appearing for the first time only now, within the melodramatic scene itself, is an even clearer source of Brahms's allusion. For it is the related countermelody that Schumann assigned to the first violins, played *dolce* as Astarte speaks Manfred's name, that matches most closely Brahms's theme (see the bottom line in Example 3.9a and compare Example 3.9b).

Given their unusual profile, the striking similarity between these themes can scarcely be attributed to coincidental uses of stylistic norms. But what finally is one to make of Brahms's appropriation? What does it mean? We can only speculate, since the composer left no verbal evidence – no "smoking gun" – that might explain the borrowing. Yet if we treat this reference as a genuine allusion, as a stylistic device leading us to consider the larger context in which the borrowed idea appears (in this case Schumann's setting of a scene from Byron's drama), then we might find some suggestive hints.

Bearing in mind that the source of Brahms's allusion is to be found less in Schumann's overture than in the *Melodram* for Manfred and Astarte, Brahms's entire secondary group, emerging in the mediant major at measure 121, might be read as a musical representation of the same dialogue. Three

Table 3.2.   Manfred addresses Astarte (= No. 10, Manfreds Ansprache an Astarte [Melodrama] in Schumann's setting)

Manfred. Hear me, hear me –	*Manfred.* O höre,
Astarte! my beloved! speak to me:	Hör' mich, Astarte! O Geliebte, sprich!
I have so much endured – so much endure –	So viel hab' ich erduldet, dulde noch –
Look on me! the grave hath not changed thee more	O sieh' mich an! das Grab hat dich nicht mehr
Than I am changed for thee. Thou lovedst me	Verwandelt, als ich dir erschein'. Du liebtest
Too much, as I loved thee: we were not made	Mich allzusehr, ich dich: wir konnten nicht
To torture thus each other, though it were	Einander so zerquälen, ob nun auch
The deadliest sin to love as we have loved.	Todsünde war die Liebe, die wir liebten.
Say that thou loath'st me not – that I do bear	O sag', dass dir nicht graut vor mir – dass ich
This punishment for both – that thou wilt be	Die Strafe für uns Beide trage – dass
One of the blessed – and that I shall die,	Den Sel'gen du gehörst – und ich dem Tode;
For hitherto all hateful things conspire	Bisher hat Alles, was ich hasse, sich
To bind me in existence – in a life	Verschworen, an das Dasein mich zu binden –
Which makes me shrink from immortality –	Ein Dasein, dass mich die Unsterblichkeit
A future like the past. I cannot rest.	Anschaudert, solchen Seins Verewigung.
I know not what I ask, nor what I seek:	Ruhlos weiss nicht ich, was ich frag' und will;
I feel but what thou art – and what I am;	Was du bist und was ich bin, fühl' ich nur,
And I would hear yet once before I perish	Und hörte gern noch einmal, eh' ich sterbe,
The voice which was my music – Speak to me!	Die Stimme, die Musik mir was, – o sprich!

For I have call'd on thee in the still night,	Gerufen hab' ich dich in stiller Nacht,
Startled the slumbering birds from the hush'd boughs	Aus Busch und Schlummer auf die Vögel scheuchend,
And woke the mountain wolves, and made the caves	Die Wölfe des Gebirgs erweck' ich, liess die Höhlen
Acquainted with thy vainly echo'd name,	Vergeblich deinen Namen widerhallen,
Which answer'd me – many things answer'd me –	Sie gaben Antwort – Antwort gaben mir
Spirits and men – but thou wert silent all.	So mancher Geist und Mensch – nur du schwiegst still.
Yet speak to me! I have outwatch'd the stars,	O sprich zu mir! Die Sterne überwacht' ich,
And gazed o'er heaven in vain in search of thee.	Gen Himmel starrend sucht ich dich vergeblich.
Speak to me! I have wander'd o'er the earth,	O sprich! Die Erde habe ich durchwandert
And never found thy likeness – Speak to me!	Und fand nie deines Gleichen. – Sprich zu mir!
Look on the fiends around – they feel for me:	Sieh' rings die Feinde wie sie mit mir fühlen.
I fear them not, and feel for thee alone.	Sie fürcht' ich nicht, und fühl' für dich allen –
Speak to me! though it be in wrath; – but say –	O sprich mit mir! sei's auch im Zorn; nur rede,

I reck not what – but let me hear thee once –	Ich rechte nicht, wovon – wenn ich dich höre –
This once – once more!	Noch einmal, nur noch einmal!

Phantom of Astarte. Manfred!	*Das Scheinbild der Astarte.* Manfred!
Manfred. Say on, say on – I live but in the sound – it is thy voice!	*Manfred.* Sprich mehr, ich leb' in deiner Stimme Ton!
A. Manfred! To-morrow ends thine earthly ills. Farewell!	*A.* Manfred, dein irdisch Leid ist morgen hin! Leb' wohl!
M. Yet one word more – am I forgiven?	*M.* Ein Wort noch! – Hast du mir verzieh'n?
A. Farewell!	*A.* Leb' wohl!
M. Say, shall we meet again?	*M.* Seh'n wir uns wieder?
A. Farewell!	*A.* Lebe wohl!
M. One word for mercy! Say, thou lovest me.	*M.* Ein Wort der Gnade, sprich, du liebst mich noch?
A. Manfred! [The Spirit of Astarte disappears.]	*A.* Manfred! [Astartes Geist verschwindet.]

Example 3.9: (a) Schumann, *Manfred*, No. 11, 53–5; (b) Brahms, First Symphony, I, secondary theme (transposed)

times the paired elements of the first-theme group are sounded, now softened in Astarte's feminine presence to reveal a milder, gentler character than before. At first, the *Schicksalsmotiv* has the upper hand, as Manfred, so to speak, poses his first two questions ("Hast du mir verzieh'n?" and "Seh'n wir uns wieder?"). But then the violins swell to prominence with an expressive quotation of what we might now term the "Manfred/Brahms" theme (even duplicating the notes D–F–D–F from its progenitor,

Example 3.10: Brahms, First Symphony, I, secondary theme

Schumann's Fourth Symphony), thereby granting special urgency to the critical third question ("Du liebst mich noch?").

The reply to that question ("Manfred!") comes in the ensuing "Astarte/Clara" melody (mm. 130–8). Significantly, Brahms seems to have encoded his own name in this tune, standing, in this reading, of course, for Manfred; the melody, after all, belongs to the same "thematic family" as the subject of the lugubrious Fugue in A♭ minor, and the composer himself, as we know, once suggested that his name could be found there (Example 3.10). Here, however, as befits the persona who speaks Manfred's name, the music is coded feminine, being inscribed *dolce* and marked by lyricism, quiet dynamics, sparse texture, and a pair of unusually attenuated "feminine" cadences (on II^6 in the antecedent; on I^6 in the consequent).[31] Although the "feminine" ending, in turn, gives birth to a new haunting call (mm. 138ff.), the familiar chromatic voice leading is never really absent, and in one hushed moment, growing out of a "purple patch" in C♭, Brahms even alludes directly to the slow chromatic passage at the beginning of Schumann's overture (compare mm. 145–8 with mm. 2–3 of the *Manfred* Overture). But that dark intrusion dissolves when the call returns in the clarinet at measure 148, nudging the harmony back to the same fragile I^6 chord with which the "Astarte/Clara" theme had originally concluded, and as the strings prolong this regained first-inversion tonic harmony (with G in the bass), before dying away on the parallel minor (with G♭ in the bass), the call is passed expressively through the wind band, thereby symbolizing the disappearance of Astarte's spirit as it trails off into the distance on the horn's low E♭.

Symphony and drama clearly diverge at this point in Brahms's score. Unlike Byron's protagonist (or Schumann's), Brahms's Manfred evidently obtains no release from his torments. When the bass descends yet another half step to F (in m. 156), the music, in a significant "misreading" of its putative source, springs back to life on a dissonant ninth chord that leads to a violent closing theme – in Manfred's key of E♭ minor, no less – in which the "Manfred/Brahms" theme is turned upside down and set off in harsh counterpoint against a line combining the *Schicksalsmotiv* – in the form of the ascending line of Schumann's "chromatic fan" (A♮–B♭–C♭) – and the iconic "fate rhythm" from Beethoven's Fifth Symphony. This is followed by an agitated close (mm. 177–85), with the formerly peaceful call made *marcato* by the horns and culminating in the first full cadence in the second group (m. 185). Four additional measures, in which the notes E♭ and G♭ are hammered out several times in succession, nail down the violent close.

The recapitulation brings no change in the mood of this ending. Although its first half is shortened considerably by the omission of the counter-statement of the first group and the beginning of the transition, its second half – comprising the crucial secondary and closing groups – remains intact. And by having the coda grow directly from its violent ending, with the familiar descending thirds let loose to expand, Brahms generates even greater drive and tension than before. It requires a brutal act to cut all this off at measure 474, and with that the music seems drained of all its energy. The descending thirds continue, to be sure, but now as a tired background to a passage (strongly reminiscent of mm. 274-94 in the development) that gradually finds its way from B♭ minor to a close in the tonic major. This cadence, when it comes at measure 495, scarcely marks the triumphant achievement of a long-sought goal, however. With its descending lines and written-out ritardando, it comes rather as an act of resignation. And in that resigned mood, the movement concludes – like the *Manfred* Overture – by reverting to a slower tempo (*Meno Allegro*), first with the chromatic motto, seemingly stuck and repeated several times over a tonic pedal on C, softly drumming out the fate rhythm, and then, just before end, with the main theme itself, now surging upward to little avail in the tonic major.

4

The middle movements

But I have my doubts about the two middle movements; as beautiful as they are in themselves, they seem to me more fitting for a serenade or suite than for an otherwise broadly scaled symphony.[1]

The middle movements (Andante sostenuto, in E major, and Un poco Allegretto e grazioso, in A♭ major) at once provide a welcome contrast to the tense opening Allegro and clear space, as it were, for the dramatic finale that is to come. It is significant in this regard that Brahms seems to have composed these less weighty movements last (perhaps as late as the summer of 1876, if Kalbeck is to be believed), only after the massive outer movements had been largely worked out. And even then, as we know, significant revisions were necessary in each before the composer was satisfied with the distribution of weight across the entire cycle.

Brahms's concern with the "unity" of the whole – with the relationship of one movement to another – is most obviously apparent in the symphony's overall tonal scheme, based on a cycle of ascending major thirds. In effect, the Andante and Allegretto form a symmetrical tonal bridge between the outer movements: (i) C minor, ending in C major–(ii) E major–(iii) A♭ major–(iv) C minor, leading to C major.[2] At the same time, as we shall discover, each contributes its share to a network of motivic cross-references that binds the whole together. Both Beethoven's Fifth and Schumann's Fourth symphonies presented obvious precedents for this technique, but Brahms is by comparison less interested in effecting simple thematic transformation than in introducing more recondite correlations, providing in this way subtle shading to the overall progression of "from darkness to light."

Second movement

Like so many of Brahms's other slow movements, the Andante sostenuto is in ternary form: A (mm. 1–27) + bridge (mm. 27–39) + B (mm. 39–66) + A′

Example 4.1: (a) Brahms, First Symphony, II, 1–2; (b) Beethoven,
Sixth Symphony, I, 1–2

(mm. 66/67–100) + coda (mm. 100–28). The head motif of the tender main
theme, with its striking emphasis on the major-third scale-degree, alludes
plainly to the beginning of Beethoven's "Pastoral" Symphony (Example 4.1),
and with that is set the movement's prevailing gentle *Stimmung*.[3] Felicitous
writing throughout for solo woodwinds (oboe, clarinet, horn) contributes
substantially to this ethos, as does the prominent use of a solo violin, whose
graceful arabesques at the end bring to mind similar passages in the *Romanze*
of Schumann's Fourth Symphony. But Brahms's pastorale is not undis-
turbed by the more troubling strains of the opening Allegro: not only the
Schicksalsmotiv, but even traces of the *Manfred* music find their way into the
main theme, bringing with them disturbing reminders of the past. And only
in the coda does the old chromatic motto give way to a diatonic version,
closely related to a passage from Wagner's *Tristan und Isolde*, with which the
movement can die away peacefully.

Notwithstanding the composer's continuing use here of allusions to
Beethoven and Schumann, his primary model seems to have been the slow
movement of Schubert's "Unfinished" Symphony, which came to light in
Vienna in 1865 and was published soon thereafter. Both Andantes, in the
same key of E major, incorporate a contrasting theme group in the
submediant (C♯ minor/D♭ major), with a light, syncopated accompaniment
supporting a beautifully meandering tune presented in turns by the oboe and
clarinet. In Schubert's hands, the secondary group evolves into a loose
passacaglia; the melody that is originally presented by the oboe and clarinet
(mm. 66ff.) is made into a bass which underpins a series of variations (mm.
96ff.). Nothing quite like that occurs in Brahms's B section; still, this idea of
transforming figure into ground (or vice versa) lies at the very heart, not only
of the central episode, but of the movement as a whole.

The opening A section offers a case in point. Although this long theme
can be understood as a kind of binary form, each of whose parts comprises a
number of discrete elements, the whole paragraph unfolds almost seamlessly
(see the left-hand column of Table 4.1). To be sure, the recurrence of the
Schicksalsmotiv in measures 5–6 (recalling the oppressive first movement)

Table 4.1

Measure	Description	Measure	Description
	PART 1		PART 1
1	Head motif, followed by	67	Head motif (somewhat disguised at first), followed by
3	half cadence in i	69	half cadence in i with
		71	cadential echo (from m. 17)
5	Digression (*Schicksalsmotiv*), with emphasis on C major, leading to	72	Digression (*Schicksalsmotiv*), with modulation to V, leading to
9	extension, followed by	76	extension and
		80	new digression (*Manfred*), followed by
13	imitative falling fifths and half cadence in i with	81	imitative falling fifths and half cadence in v and
17	cadential echo		
		85	new digression (*Manfred*), leading to
		87	full (but attenuated) cadence in V, elided to
	PART 2		PART 2
17/18	Oboe melody (m) on V	90/91	Oboe melody (m) on V
20	(m) repeated	93	(m) repeated
22	(m) + head motif in bass, leading to	95	(m´) + head motif in bass, leading to
24	interrupted half cadence, followed by	97	interrupted half cadence, followed by
25	renewed drive to	98	renewed drive to
26–7	full cadence in I	99–100	full cadence in I

and the subsequent loud and jagged display of C major harmony (the ultimate tonal goal of the entire symphony) are disruptive; but these "intrusions" are prepared by the chromatic voice leading and augmented-sixth harmony of the preceding half cadence in the tonic minor (mm. 3–4), and the whole digression is made to emerge into and recede from the on-going theme by means of a crescendo and decrescendo. The only real break occurs in measure 17, when the first period (ending, again, on a half cadence in the tonic minor) yields to the oboe's contrasting lyrical tune (beginning on dominant harmony). But in a process that is begun five measures later the two parts soon become completely interwoven, as the head motif recurs as a bass line in the strings and leads to a resumption in the foreground of the original cadential material, now interrupted and only after a repeated effort brought to a full close in the tonic major.

Elided to this cadence is the bridge (mm. 27–39). This paragraph, like the A section that precedes it, embodies both an echo of the *Schicksalsmotiv* (in the ascending chromatic voice leading that begins in m. 29) and an anticipation of the finale (whose slow introduction and coda include a recollection of the appoggiatura motif occurring several times in mm. 31–2). Figure and ground are set in sharp relief at the beginning: to the first violins' ascending, initially unaccompanied melody is added a neutral (albeit related) background consisting of a repeated dotted motif in the second violins and violas. Yet this accompanimental idea is soon transformed into the very melody that it had originally accompanied (beginning in m. 31). To be sure, the first violins maintain the melodic interest for the time being, soaring to new heights by means of a series of expressive appoggiature. Upon the arrival on a climactic tonic $^6_4$ in the key of C♯ minor, however, the second violins and violas emerge as fully equal partners with the first violins in a brief passage of double counterpoint (mm. 34–5), after which the music hastens to a strong half close in the new key.

When the oboe breaks into this cadence with the sustained first note of what turns out to be the contrasting B tune (upbeat to m. 39), it initiates still another quicksilver passage in which Brahms plays on the relation between figure and ground. Embodied within the strings' accompaniment to the oboe's tune is a surprising recollection of the head motif of the movement's main theme (Table 4.2). At first the notes recur unchanged melodically (beginning on G♯), but harmonized, after the example of the slow movements in Schubert's last two piano sonatas, in the new third-related key (i.e., beginning on $\hat{5}$ instead of $\hat{3}$). With the appearance of the clarinet in measure 42 on a long-held E♭, the music begins to turn toward the local dominant, A♭ major. It is not merely the tonality of the ensuing third movement that is anticipated here, however: when, in measure 44, the clarinet quits its sustained E♭ and moves down by step to D♭ and C, it adumbrates, in a fleeting moment, the Allegretto's main theme (likewise scored for clarinet), doing so over an accompaniment that now, in anticipation of the unusual form of that later theme – whose two five-measure phrases are related by exact intervallic inversion – pulsates with a mirror form of the head motif.

Table 4.2

Measure	Description
39	tune in oboe in C♯ minor (vi), accompanied at first by head motif of main theme (with original notes G♯–A–C♯–B♯–A–G♯ treated as $\hat{5}$–$\hat{6}$–$\hat{1}$–$\hat{7}$–$\hat{6}$–$\hat{5}$ in new key), and leading to
43	tonicization of A♭ as tune is taken up by clarinet (with foreshadowing of main theme of third movement), accompanied at first by inversion of head motif of main theme (C–B♭–G–A♭–B♭♭ = $\hat{3}$–$\hat{2}$–$\hat{7}$–$\hat{1}$–♭$\hat{2}$ in new key), and then pushing toward
47	cadence in D♭ major (VI), with continuation in clarinet joined by return of tune in lower strings (now embodying reference to chromatic retransition of first movement), accompanying head motif and interrupted half cadence from end of main theme (F–G♭–B♭–A♭–G♭–F / E♭–E♭–E♭–F♭–D♭ = $\hat{3}$–$\hat{4}$–$\hat{6}$–$\hat{5}$–$\hat{4}$–$\hat{3}$ / $\hat{2}$–$\hat{2}$–$\hat{2}$–♭$\hat{3}$–$\hat{1}$ in new key), leading to enharmonic modulation and
53	completion of half cadence in C♯ minor, with tune resumed by strings, leading to motivic fragmentation and dissolution

Before long the roles of figure and ground are called once more into question. In measure 47, the clarinet (soon to be joined by the other woodwinds) offers new, slower paced melodic material leading to a cadence in D♭, while the B theme finds itself removed to the bass line, and the strings, in between, continue their syncopated "accompaniment," but now assuming greater thematic prominence than before and presenting virtually the whole of the main theme (beginning on $\hat{3}$ in D♭). The implied half cadence is interrupted, however, and the dominant is not reached until measure 53, where – as if to obliterate all distinction between figure and ground – the orchestra sounds a loud G♯ in several octaves. A final statement of the theme follows, mostly loud and again in C♯ minor, but this soon breaks down into motivic fragments that dissolve quietly into a ii$^{\circ6}_{5}$ chord in measures 65–6.

The reprise of the A theme (mm. 66/67ff.) emerges subtly against a continuing background of quiet timpani roll and an impressive melody played in three octaves by the upper strings. At first the head motif, harmonized and sustained quietly in the upper woodwinds, remains half hidden; only as the string melody descends into a lower register (m. 68) does the "real" theme come into relief. But this is not the most significant difference between the A and A′ sections (see Table 4.1). In the restatement,

Example 4.2: (a) II, 80–1; (b) II, 84–7

the digression involving the *Schicksalsmotiv* avoids the earlier emphasis on C major, the triumphant goal of the symphony, and instead modulates to the dominant, B major, in which key the first part comes to a close in measure 90.

This tonal surprise is marked by two strange thematic digressions. Both, tellingly, return us to the troubled world of Byron's *Manfred*.[4] Indeed, the first digression (mm. 80–1) derives from the entire family of "Manfred themes" that were discussed in Chapter 3 (Example 4.2a). In its tonal disposition, with descending chromatic line beginning on F♯, this passage betrays its origin in Schumann's melodramatic setting of the critical dialogue between Manfred and Astarte to which Brahms had alluded in the second theme of the opening Allegro (cf. Example 3.9a); at the same time, its paired, descending three-note motifs recall the beginnings of both the "Astarte theme" of Schumann's *Manfred* Overture and the related subject of Brahms's Fugue in A♭ Minor for Organ (cf. Examples 3.7 and 3.10).

This quiet digression, stealing into the narrative flow as a kind of fleeting recollection of the distant past, quickly evaporates; but only a few moments later, in measures 84/5–87, the same experience recurs in the memory, now rather asserting itself in a second digression based on similar material (Example 4.2b). This time the descending chromatic line supports a transformation of the "Astarte" theme's characteristic up-and-down melodic line, and by concluding with a drawn-out arpeggiation of the same inscrutable e♯°⁷ chord that had accompanied Astarte's disappearance in Schumann's melodramatic scene (see No. 10, four measures after letter T), Brahms not only clinches the allusion but seems to reopen an important, if painful question.

In the first movement, as I have argued, the young Brahms pointedly "misread" Manfred's encounter with the spirit of Astarte: to judge from the oppressive closing group that follows his allusion there, at any rate, Brahms's Manfred had remained a tormented soul, finding no peace in Astarte's forgiveness; even the coda, with its conclusion in C major, offers only a glimmer of hope. By the time many years later when the second movement

Example 4.3: (a) Wagner, Concert Ending of the Prelude to *Tristan und Isolde*, 109a; (b) Brahms, First Symphony, II, 105–6

came to be written, however, Brahms might reflect more dispassionately on the matter, and the same allusion might be put to purposes more in keeping with Byron's poem.

Thus, as the reprise of the A section concludes (from m. 90), the solo oboe is joined for its tune by the first horn and an expressive solo violin. Both instruments play crucial roles also in the coda (mm. 100ff.), in which the same oboe melody is transposed to begin on the tonic and includes a suitable emphasis on the subdominant. The first two phrases, in which the tune is carried by the first horn, supporting graceful arabesques in the solo violin, recur largely as before; the third phrase, however, offers some new twists – and with that a subtle allusion to the Concert Ending of the Prelude to *Tristan und Isolde*, with its references to the concluding *Transfiguration* music (Example 4.3).[5] Lacking Wagner's expressive dissonance on the first note, Brahms's tender melody knows little of the erotic sound of its source; yet the two themes otherwise show remarkably similar profiles, descending through the major scale from $\hat{2}$ to $\hat{5}$ in nearly identical rhythm and with a comparable appoggiatura figure coming at the end. And by alternating his theme between flute and violins Brahms even evokes Wagner's back-and-forth deployment of clarinet and violins.

But whereas Wagner proceeds quickly to his remarkable final cadence, in which the famous Love–Death motif of ascending chromatic steps is transfigured over minor subdominant harmony into a glorious ascent of three diatonic ones (Example 4.4a), Brahms indulges in a wayward passage, based on Wagner's sensuous descending line, that eventually winds down with a thematic extension in the solo violin and first clarinet. Following an elided cadence in measure 114 the bridge figure is taken up once more, leading to a beautiful reappearance of the *Schicksalsmotiv*, with edges softened by the participation of the solo violin and extended now into a lovely feminine cadence. A recurrence of the bridge figure leads again to *Schicksalsmotiv*. Here, however, Brahms works a more dramatic transformation than before, completing at last the interrupted allusion to Wagner's Concert Ending (Example 4.4b): now, as in the model, the ascending voice leading is made

Example 4.4: (a) Wagner, Concert Ending of the Prelude to *Tristan und Isolde*, 114a–16a; (b) Brahms, First Symphony, II, 122–4

diatonic ($\hat{1}$–$\hat{2}$–$\hat{3}$), and the music unfolds over the same minor subdominant that had marked the similar plagal cadence with which Wagner had ended. Here, indeed, is Brahms's *Liebestod*.[6] And to recognize that the ensuing arpeggiation of the tonic chord in the pizzicato strings recalls, not only Wagner's concluding arpeggio for harp, but also the ending of the serene slow movement of the C Minor Piano Quartet – likewise in E major, and likewise composed many years after the turbulent, autobiographically in-flected first movement – is only to recognize something of the larger significance of this catharsis. Faint echoes of the *Schicksalsmotiv* are still to be heard in the symphony, as part of its abstract narrative progression; but the *Manfred* music, with all its personal connotations, does not recur.

Third movement

The third movement (Un poco Allegretto e grazioso, A♭, $\frac{2}{4}$) is no real scherzo. It is rather more comparable, as Richard Pohl noted in his review of the first two performances, "to a sweet idyll, which emerges as an Intermezzo, as a brief sunny respite, only to disappear again."[7] None the less, the music does contain healthy doses of the playful element that lies at the heart of the scherzo style, and its design is most readily understood in terms of the simple ternary form that is traditionally associated with that genre.[8]

The opening Allegretto (mm. 1–70) unfolds a kind of rounded binary form, in which the first main section, beginning in A♭ but quickly modulating to the dominant, is given a varied repetition, while the second section, beginning in F minor at measure 45, is heard only once (thus AA′ + BA″). Moreover, the A material is severely truncated when it returns at the end, and the music quickly dissolves to a close, not in the tonic, but in the dominant, E♭. Next comes the trio (L'istesso tempo, B major, $\frac{6}{8}$), featuring a lively exchange between repeated-note triplets in the winds and descending triadic figures in the strings. Like the Allegretto, this section is in rounded binary form with a written-out repetition of the opening part; but it also incorporates a complete repetition of the second part (thus AA′ + BA″ BA″) and, after building to a brilliant climax, with trumpets joining the horns and woodwinds, comes to a vigorous full close. Although the Allegretto is resumed soon thereafter, what follows is not a simple *da capo*. As we learned in Chapter 2, Brahms struggled over the proportions of this final section, and in the end he included a rather abbreviated restatement of the opening material, followed by a brief coda (based on the trio).

Within its relatively straightforward ternary design, this piece offers more than its share of formal sophistication; it is, as Tovey remarked, "one of those terse and highly organized movements which are so short that contemporary criticism frequently fails to see that they are on a symphonic scale at all."[9] Indeed, Brahms gives the impression of a larger scale than might otherwise be the case, not only by withholding closure in the tonic from the opening Allegretto, but by welding all three main sections of the movement into a single continuous piece. The descending triadic figure that characterizes the one side of the trio's dialogue between strings and winds, for example, grows directly from the descending triad on E♭ with which the preceding Allegretto had come to its nebulous conclusion (mm. 67–71ff.). By the same token, the triplets that mark the other side lead back from the trio to the Allegretto, where they continue for some time as a new background for the returning main theme (mm. 108–15ff.).[10]

But much of the interest of the music results from Brahms's playful handling of elements within the main theme itself (mm. 1–18), a contrasting double period that contains certain surprises which have their effect throughout the entire course of the movement. The first period, which presents a smooth and graceful melody played by the clarinet over light accompaniment, comprises an opening phrase that ends with a half cadence in the tonic, followed by an exact inversion that comes round to a half cadence in the dominant. Although Brahms might easily have bound the two phrases together in a conventional structure of 4 measures + 4 measures, instead he dwells slightly on the final note of each, thereby extending the phrase for an additional measure, and so providing its ending with a special emphasis – and one that is only enhanced by the quiet swell that is brought to the moment by the first violins (mm. 4–6 and 9–11). By contrast, in the second period, consisting of a pair of four-measure tutti phrases with dotted rhythms, the surprise results from Brahms's treatment of harmonic implication. Although this passage moves strongly toward a full cadence in the dominant, E♭, it stops just short of its goal: in measure 17 the I_4^6 chord in the new key is transformed into a V[7] harmony in the old, and in that way the music is nudged back to the tonic, A♭.

Yet, having thus marked the opening material in our consciousness with certain affective moments, Brahms proceeds to confound our expectations by never again repeating it in the same way. For example, in the counterstatement of the opening A section (mm. 19–44) the last note of each of the first two phrases, which we now expect to be extended for one measure, is extended instead for three, during which Brahms introduces chromatic voice leading that brings to mind, even in the midst of this bucolic Intermezzo, the *Schicksalsmotiv* from the first movement (mm. 22–5 and 29–32). Once more the continuation (beginning at m. 33) seems headed toward a cadence in E♭; but once more this implication is thwarted – not, as before, by the failure of a I_4^6 chord to resolve properly (indeed, in m. 39–40 it progresses dutifully to V[7]) but by the subsequent failure of that dominant-seventh chord to complete the implied cadence. Instead its B♭ root becomes the bass of a G♭[6] triad, which (acting as the Neapolitan in F minor) sets into motion a transition to the B section. And when the primary theme recurs once more at the end of the opening Allegretto, it is shorn of all but its opening phrase. Again Brahms plays tricks with the extension of the last note, which now runs to five measures and this time incorporates, first in the clarinet and then in the violins, a descending E♭ triad, which had originally served to link the A and A′ sections (mm. 18–19) but which now, as mentioned already, serves to make a smooth transition into the trio.

The principal theme makes only two appearances, finally, in the abbreviated *da capo* (mm. 115–53). The opening phrase returns at the outset. Again the tune, now set off against a background of triplets maintained from the trio, is carried by the clarinet; and again the first violins steal into the texture to emphasize the sustained last note. Yet this time the violins do not yield back to the clarinet for the inverted phrase; they proceed instead with a significant new variation (*molto dolce*), to which we shall shortly return. In its last appearance (beginning at m. 144) the primary theme departs even further from its original shape. Here the melody is sounded in stark octaves in the lower register, and, as the violas, cellos, and double basses get stuck on the tune's characteristic turning figure, the violins make a final reference to the *Schicksalsmotiv*. The ensuing brief epilogue (mm. 154–64) maintains this

Example 4.5: III, 109–15

new, darker atmosphere. As Julius Harrison described it, "[p]hrases once so vigorous in the B major section now become inert and dark in colouring in what is nevertheless a beautiful coda: one admittedly melancholic in Brahms's way, yet one that demonstrates convincingly that unfailing unity of thought which, like some bridge, carries this movement over to the next one."[11]

As we saw in Chapter 2, Brahms indicated that he had made a "drastic shortening" in this movement because "the finale demanded ... consideration." Raymond Knapp, assuming that this remark applied not only to the movement at hand but to the Andante as well (which he further assumed to have originally been a complete sonata form), has speculated that the composer's intent in shortening the two movements was not merely to reduce their duration, but to undercut their thematic and harmonic completion, thereby helping to ensure the pre-eminence of the finale.[12] That explanation becomes doubtful, however, when we recognize, as I have argued, that the Andante evidently was never in sonata form (though it certainly was revised) nor even shortened very much.

We might arrive at a somewhat different explanation if we assume instead that Brahms's comment about shortening the music applied only to the Allegretto. Clearly, the relationship between the third and fourth movements was a matter of some significance. The "bridge" between the two is nearly palpable: the descending C minor tetrachord with which the finale begins seems to emerge directly out of the descending quiet A♭ triad, in the same lower strings, with which the Intermezzo ends. But that link is only one in a larger chain of motivic relationships (Example 4.5). Brahms had in fact already introduced a descending tetrachord, beginning on E♭, in the passage that leads the trio back to the Allegretto (mm. 109ff.). At first this pattern is heard enharmonically in B major, the key of the trio. Then, upon repetition, it sounds, as written, in A♭ minor. Finally, after a third statement, transposed stepwise down to D♭, it is transformed into the head motif of the returning clarinet melody (in A♭ major). Nor is the descending tetrachord the only idea from the finale that is anticipated here. When, at measure 120, the violins spell the clarinet with their unexpected new variation of the main tune, they

Example 4.6: III, 45–7; (b) III, 53–5; (c) IV, 13–14; (d) IV, 1–2, 118–19, 128–30

actually adumbrate a salient motif in the finale's main theme, indeed, the very motif that most closely echoes the *Freudenthema* (e.g., compare mm. 120 and 122 in the third movement with mm. 70ff. in the finale).

But the *absence* in the reprise of certain material – the B section (mm. 45–61 in the opening Allegretto) fails to recur – might be no less significant in this regard. Consider the clarinet melody beginning in measure 46 (Example 4.6a). The head motif of this descending scalar pattern not only recurs in measures 53–55 as a counterpoint in the bass to a rough inversion of the tune in the flute and oboe (Example 4.6b); it also anticipates important material in the finale (Example 4.6c–d). With its distinctive augmented second, B♮–A♭, it foreshadows the head motif of the finale's main theme as it appears in C minor in the slow introduction (mm. 13–14). At the same time it adumbrates the descending tetrachord from C to G that sets the finale into motion and recurs later in that movement as an ostinato bass in the secondary group (mm. 118ff.). Indeed, as that secondary group unfolds, the ostinato figure is transposed and otherwise varied, eventually achieving a shape that directly recalls the distinctive guise of the original clarinet melody, with an augmented second between the second and third notes (mm. 129–30). Important, too, in this regard is the tantalizing anticipation of the key of the finale (C major) in the sudden tutti outbursts in mm. 50–3.

Hints of the last movement, then, are to be found in abundance, both in the B section of the opening Intermezzo and in the rewritten, truncated reprise. In view of that, we might now imagine why, in the end, Brahms apparently decided to sacrifice the returning B section, with its welter of thematic and tonal anticipations of the movement to come. Perhaps he concluded that to do otherwise would be to risk overpriming the pump. It was time now to begin the finale itself.

5

Structure and meaning in the last movement

The immensely towering finale shows the freedom with which the symphonic form can be handled if it grows organically from ideas that are capable of being developed. Nothing of the routine can be traced there.[1]

One fundamental difference, however, must not be overlooked: Beethoven was an idealist and a convinced optimist; the optimistic philosophy of the Rationalists, as expressed in Leibniz's faith in "the best of all possible worlds," remained alive in him, as it did in Schiller. How far Brahms, the skeptical pessimist of the late nineteenth century, was removed from this conception! The hymnlike enthusiasm of his finale lacks the ultimate in genuine, convinced, and convincing joy. The jubilation with which the movement comes to a close is the result of a self-delusion. One can sense in it more the desire to be joyful than real surrender to joy.[2]

I

The dramatic slow introduction to Brahms's finale – like the ferocious opening of the last movement of Beethoven's Ninth – immediately restores the tragic mood of the opening movement, which is recalled by the dark key of C minor and similar uses of chromaticism, orchestration, instrumentation, and expressive gesture. As Tovey noted, Brahms brings forth in this Adagio "all the future materials [of the ensuing Allegro] in a magnificent cloudy procession, as in the first movement, but on a larger scale and with far more human terror and expectation."[3] Thus the opening measures anticipate both the head motif of the primary theme and the descending tetrachord that later undergirds the secondary group. At measure 6 the pizzicato strings attempt to break loose from the prevailing gloomy mood, in a passage that looks ahead to the development; yet, despite the marked *stringendo* and rising register, this effort is unsuccessful: the strings are left hanging on the Neapolitan sixth, and at measure 12 the winds usher in a condensed reprise of the entire opening. The oboe attempts a third statement of the descending tetrachord in measure 20, but the lower strings interrupt with rising scales much like those later used in the transition (mm. 106ff.); the winds follow at measure 22 with a restless idea, related to gestures heard in the first and second movements, and one that is destined to recur both as the closing subject (mm. 148ff.) and, sublimely transformed, in the coda (mm. 417ff.). This music soon builds to a frightening outbreak of diminished-seventh chords, and when in measure 28 the last of these is broken off by an ominous drum-roll on the tonic, leaving only a stark residual minor third (A–C) sounding in the lower register, the darkness and terror seem inextinguishable.

But the drum-roll soon fades, and as the bass completes its stepwise descent to the dominant, C minor yields unequivocally to C major (m. 30, Più Andante). Day breaks to the comforting voice of the alphorn theme, sounded against a luminous background of quiet trombones (making their first appearance in the symphony) and muted tremolando strings. Here, in a passage whose effect, as Raymond Knapp has observed, can be likened to that of Beethoven's recitative "O Freunde, nicht diese Töne!," the "negative" key of C minor and its associated chromatic voice leading is finally dispelled.[4] This is no false hint of the tonic major, like those that had occurred in each of the preceding movements, but an announcement of a lasting "positive" change. And when we recognize that the opening stepwise descending third of the alphorn theme had been anticipated in the Adagio (mm. 20–1 in the oboe and clarinet; mm. 24–6 in the first violins; and mm. 27–8 in the woodwinds and first violins), the sense of transcendence occurring when the theme emerges whole in the solo horn is only emphasized. At measure 47 the trombones take center stage with a brief solemn chorale. But this soon yields to a return of the alphorn theme, intensified at first by means of overlapping entries before beautifully expiring into a quiet half cadence and general pause.

What follows, as the primary theme of a magnificent Allegro, is the broad strophic melody in C major that has forever been likened to the *Freudenthema* from Beethoven's Ninth. Most early reviewers took note of the obvious similarities – the melody not only bears a certain family resemblance to the "Joy" theme but even seems to quote from it – but few thought to take the allusion for anything more than a simple sign of the composer's characteristic (and predictable) stylistic orientation in the work; some less charitable critics even imagined it to represent a defect in Brahms's own originality.

More recent writers, by and large, have played down the significance of Brahms's allusion. Tovey, for example, argued that "the melody is great enough to stand on its own merits," adding that the one near-quotation of the *Freudenthema*, coming at precisely the moment in Brahms's tune where "the essential meaning and harmony are most original," was a distraction and ought simply to be forgotten. Michael Musgrave likewise has made little of the allusion, not only because he finds a handful of other models for Brahms's theme, but because the one "tangible thematic link" between the two melodies seems to him to form an "incidental rather than essential relationship."[5] Yet Brahms never denied the presence of an echo of the Ninth Symphony, and we would do better to read his well-known remark about "every jackass" who took note of the similarity, not as an indication that the allusion was of little consequence, but as a wholly typical "defense mechanism" against the kind of broader exploration of his compositional workshop that a more forthcoming attitude would have invited.[6]

A similar attempt at using a blunt "confession" as a means of deflecting any serious discussion of the kind is evident in another case of thematic allusion that dates from the same period. George Henschel reported that at Saßnitz in July 1876 the composer asked for advice on how he might acknowledge that the theme of one of his recent songs ("Unüberwindlich," Op. 72, No. 5) had been adapted from a certain work by Domenico Scarlatti (the Sonata in D Major, K. 223/L. 214). Then in May 1877, when the song was being readied for the engraver, Brahms explained to Simrock that because the theme in question was "fremdes Eigenthum" it would require special handling. At first Brahms thought it would be sufficient merely to have the passage set off in a bracket marked ⌊*alienum*⌋, but a few days later he decided that the original composer should actually be named: "[I] ask for ⌊*D. Scarlatti*⌋. It is only because it's often thought I also use folk melodies."[7]

The ironic intent here – of Brahms's language certainly and perhaps even his acknowledging gesture itself – is clear, and it does not seem unlikely that the "folk melody" that he had most in mind was in fact Beethoven's *Freudenthema*, the source of his most recent and notorious thematic allusion. The First Symphony, at any rate, had cemented his reputation for making such extra-compositional references. An anonymous reviewer for the *Neue Zeitschrift für Musik* put it thus in his report on the first Viennese performance (17 December 1876):

A young composer can be forgiven when he adheres to great models; Brahms has done as much up to now, in his first sonatas (e.g., compare the scherzo in his Sonata Op. 5 with the last movement of Mendelssohn's C minor trio), as well as in his later works. But eventually the dependence on others must be given up for once and room be made for greater artistic independence, if the artist is to become truly significant for us! Brahms's symphony seems unfortunately to resemble rather more an arrangement of motifs from Beethoven, Schumann, and Wagner than a product created independently from the innermost self, and because of that it will never be able to captivate our interest to the same degree as do the works of those masters.[8]

And in a brief report on the first Berlin performance of the work (11 November 1877), Wilhelm Tappert confirmed this aspect of Brahms's public image in his own backhanded way as he scoffed at the "lamentable and even laughable attempt to prove that Brahms had 'pilfered' all his melodic motifs." Indeed, holding the very position that Tappert had sought to discredit, an anonymous reviewer of the first performances in New York and Boston (December 1877) made the striking observation that Brahms's works all "seem filled from beginning to end with resemblances to familiar themes."[9]

It is in the light of such reports that we must read Adolf Schubring's humorous response to Brahms's recent borrowings, which is found in an unpublished letter of 9 October 1877 that was sent just at the time when, as Schubring knew, the composer was proof-reading the symphony:

Let's imagine that you hadn't marked the theme [in "Unüberwindlich"] as being by Scarlatti and some dumb Leipzig prophet had spontaneously discovered it "as a plagiarism"; what throat clearing and whispering would have resulted! Now that through the indication "Scarlatti" you have explained the allusion as *intended*, no one can hold anything against you. How would it be if you do just the same thing in the case of the main theme of the last movement of the C Minor Symphony, and in the score and piano edition confess that an "Homage à Beethoven et Schumann" was *intended*? You won't believe what criminal charges the little Beethoven reminiscence from the Ninth has brought you in Leipzig; if Bernsdorf [Eduard Bernsdorf, a critic for the *Signale für die musikalische Welt*] or consorts had also found that even the first half of the theme is almost literally the forgotten (by others but not by me) Schumann/Becker "Rheinlied," then it would have been entirely clear to Bernsdorf that you are a completely untalented maker of epigonal products of the fifth order. You will cut all these silly writers off short if over it you write "⌊*Schumann*⌋ ⌊*Beethoven*⌋." In case you don't know Schumann's "Rheinlied" [WoO 1], I'll set out the beginning for you here:

Sie sol - len ihn nicht ha - ben, den frei - en deutsch-en Rhein,

Perhaps this letter will meet you just when you are proof-reading the 4th movement.[10]

Although intended in jest, Schubring's notion of a kind of "double allusion" in Brahms's main theme was in fact on the mark, and it brings us back to the question of the work's genesis.

As we saw in Chapter 2, a significant breakthrough in the compositional process of the last movement seems to have been made in the summer of 1874. To judge from the ostinato-based secondary group of the completed finale, we might assume that Brahms's recent preoccupation with Baroque ground-bass technique, as displayed in both the finale of the *Haydn Variations* and the composer's subsequent study of several ostinato movements by J. S. Bach and Buxtehude, had played a decisive role in this advance. Clearly central to Brahms's project was Bach's Cantata No. 150 ("Nach dir, Herr, verlanget mich"), in whose final chorus, as Philipp Spitta had noted in the same letter of 9 February 1874 in which he had also encouraged the composer to complete his symphony, Bach had taken the unlikely step of adapting the genre of the ciacona, which had originally been a dance, into the realm of vocal music.[11]

Brahms's most immediate compositional response to Bach's unusual strategy took shape, to be sure, not in the massive symphonic finale (which would require another two years' labor), but in a little piece that came far more easily that summer. In the last of *Neue Liebeslieder Wälzer*, Op. 65 (a setting of Goethe's "Nun, ihr Musen, genug!" and entitled here simply "Zum Schluß"), Brahms undergirded the vocal quartet with a basso ostinato in the four-hand piano accompaniment, thereby characteristically combining Bach's innovation in Cantata No. 150 with a return to the genre's origins within the dance.[12]

Yet a similar restoration of "generic propriety" is evident in the finale of Brahms's symphony, with its notorious echo of Beethoven's setting of Schiller's "Ode to Joy." As Friedrich Chrysander noted, in his review of an early Hamburg performance, Brahms, far from making a "weak and unproductive imitation" of his Beethovenian model, had essayed here something of "art-historical significance," intending nothing less than "to create a counterpart to the last sections of the Ninth Symphony that would achieve the same effect in nature and intensity without calling on the assistance of song," in short, effecting a "return of the symphony that mixes playing and singing to the purely instrumental symphony."[13]

Chrysander's account rings true as far as it goes, but it does not tell the entire story. For, as suggested above, Brahms's main theme contains a significant "double allusion," one involving not only Beethoven's finale but, of equal significance, an ostinato chorale movement by Bach. Indeed, the

Freudenthema is not echoed until the third measure of Brahms's melody and comes to dominate that tune only in its second half; the famous head motif (already anticipated in the opening measures of the slow introduction) seems to be related instead to the distinctive ground bass from Bach's chorus "Ach, Herr! lehre uns bedenken," from Cantata No. 106 ("Gottes Zeit ist die allerbeste Zeit") (Example 5.1). This remarkable "Homage à Beethoven et Bach" provides the key to unlocking a good deal of the symphony's meaning; but before we can make much sense of it we must take up the matter of the movement's unusual form.

II

Although most critics would agree that the "generic dominant" of the finale is sonata form, agreement can quickly break down over the question of how to understand its departures from some of the most fundamental norms of that genre. Representative is the recent skirmish over the matter between Giselher Schubert and Reinhold Brinkmann. Schubert, taking the more traditional position, holds that the movement contains two large parts, unfolded as essentially a sonata form without development (but with a developmental reprise); by contrast, Brinkmann, in a new reading, maintains that the movement comprises a kind of three-part sonata form (but with the alphorn theme displacing the main theme from the recapitulation).[14]

We might begin to find our way out of this thicket by recognizing that the movement, however modified, cannot easily be reduced to any single "textbook form": it is precisely in the "modifications" that the greatest interest lies. A more flexible and instructive approach to the movement is suggested by James Hepokoski's recent work on Strauss's *Don Juan* and the Symphony No. 5 by Sibelius. Indeed, Brahms's finale shares with these later pieces a similar tendency toward what Hepokoski terms "deformation," that is, the unfolding of a "nonnormative individual structure ... that contravenes some of the most central defining traditions, or default gestures, of a genre while explicitly retaining others."[15]

In this view, Brahms's finale can be seen to combine aspects of at least three different "sonata deformations." The most obvious is what Hepokoski calls the "Brahmsian deformation," familiar from its use in many other movements by the composer, in which a conventional (albeit unrepeated) sonata-form exposition is followed, first, by a recapitulation in the tonic key of all or a part of the main theme (as in a sonata-rondo), then by a passage that has the hallmarks of a true sonata-form development, and finally by a

Example 5.1: (a) J. S. Bach, Cantata No. 106, II, 48–50, 59–60; (b) Beethoven, Ninth Symphony, IV, 124–7; (c) Brahms, First Symphony, IV, 1–3, 61–3; (d) Brahms, First Symphony, IV, 61–78

resumption of the recapitulation that had been broken off earlier.[16] In this case, the exposition (mm. 62–183) is followed by a second section consisting of the recapitulation of the main theme (mm. 185ff.), development (from around m. 204), and recapitulation of the second and closing groups (mm. 302ff.).

Yet – what is unusual in this formal type – the development is itself briefly deformed by a sudden return to recapitulatory material (from m. 220 to around m. 230). Moreover – what is ultimately more significant – the entire "Brahmsian deformation" is subjected to two additional deformations. Thus the dramatic "breakthrough" of the alphorn theme at measure 285, coming as the culmination of a goal-directed process of developmental intensification, effectively displaces the main theme (or the "Beethovenian" portions, at any rate) from any further significant role in the movement.

And that reorientation is only enhanced by the equally dramatic recollection of the trombone chorale at the very end of the piece (mm. 407–16), which strengthens the growing impression of a subordinated sonata form by the creation of an encasing "introduction-coda frame."

Brinkmann, in an impressive recent account, has related these striking deformations to larger historical issues concerning Brahms's creative encounter with what he calls "a [significant] Beethovenian matrix, that 'plot-archetype' of nineteenth-century symphonic music which might be paraphrased as the resolution of a conflict of ideas through an inner formal process aimed toward a liberating ending – in a nutshell, the 'positive' overcoming of a 'negative' principle."[17] Brahms's intention to take up this matrix is of course made evident in both the overall tonal trajectory of his symphony (moving from C minor to C major, as in Beethoven's Fifth) and his allusion to the *Freudenthema* in the great hymn-like theme of his own finale.

Beethoven's fulfillment of the plot-archetype is essentially unproblematic and accords well with the great ideas of his age: both the C major march that ends the Fifth Symphony and the choral setting of Schiller's "Ode to Joy" concluding the Ninth are aesthetic expressions of a humanity which seemed destined, on the promises of the French Revolution, to find a new and better condition. But as a child of a later era that followed decades of restoration and was marked by a consolidation of conservative forces in society – of an era in which the optimism of Beethoven's time had yielded to inwardness and melancholy – Brahms could scarcely share the earlier composer's goal. This is evident, holds Brinkmann, in the two deformations under question. At the central point of the formal discourse, where the intensifying development at last gives way to the recapitulation, the main theme is displaced as the *dramatis persona* by the alphorn theme; and in the coda, where, especially in view of the rondo-like elements of the form, one might expect another statement of the main theme, the trombone chorale returns instead. Twice, therefore, the movement's primary subject is "effaced" by a theme that is more in keeping with the pessimistic *Weltanschauung* of the later nineteenth century. In the end the theme that had alluded to Beethoven's great musical icon of freedom – that symbol "of change, reformulation, new foundation, even ... utopia" – withdraws, to be displaced by representations of Nature (the alphorn theme) and Religion (the trombone chorale), realms containing higher powers that are "beyond history, unchanging, constant, essentially at rest."[18]

Brinkmann seems to be on the right path here, although we can fruitfully broaden the context still further. For one thing, considering the evident relation of Brahms's main theme to the ostinato bass from Bach's funeral cantata, it would be misguided to essentialize the subject as simply a "Joy theme." In addition, the main theme is not really "effaced" in the later portions of the movement; the "Beethovenian" echoes disappear, to be sure, but, as we shall see, the "Bachian" head motif continues to figure prominently right up to the end. At the same time, it is important not to overlook the links between the unusual formal features of Brahms's finale and two pivotal works in the *post-Beethoven* symphonic tradition: Schubert's "Great" C Major Symphony and the Symphony No. 2 of Schumann.

As noted already by the anonymous reviewer of the first American performances of the symphony, the alphorn theme recalls the beautiful melody that opens Schubert's slow introduction, with which, indeed, it shares a range of significant attributes, including key, instrumentation, and even a characteristic cadential figure.[19] Moreover, as Constantin Floros has argued, the same melody by Schubert shares a certain resemblance with Beethoven's *Freudenthema* and so also with the *main theme* of Brahms's finale. Each of the three tunes is a kind of hymn, whose character is delineated by a diatonic cantabile melodic structure, flowing rhythm, and clear-cut periodicity, and all three undergo progressively richer scoring with each strophic-like repetition.[20] In most respects Brahms held more closely than did Schubert to the Beethovenian model, above all by reserving the hymn for the finale, where it appears in consequence of a turbulent introduction. Yet Brahms also borrowed directly from Schubert within his main theme: the pizzicato accompaniment provided in the first two strophes (mm. 62–93) relates directly to the similar setting found in the middle of Schubert's introduction (mm. 9–28).

A broader relationship to Schubert's last symphony – not only the first great post-Beethoven symphony, as Brahms knew, but a work to be reckoned with on its own terms, too – is established by a host of subsequent allusions. Most obvious, the exposition's tonal plan of C major–G major–E minor recalls Schubert's three-key exposition of C major–E minor–G major. Moreover, Brahms follows the earlier composer's typical practice of arriving at the second group by means of a *coup de théâtre*. To be sure, the transition moves forcefully enough toward the dominant (actually arriving in the key of V/V by m. 111). But all that is given up only two measures later, when the music unexpectedly reverts to the tonic, the arrival of which is marked by the introduction of a significant new dotted rhythmic figure on the notes C and G that alludes to the main theme of the "Great" C Major. And when at

71

measure 118 the second group does emerge at last, following two hasty overlapping recollections of the alphorn theme, it embraces an ostinato bass that recalls, not only the descending tetrachord with which the movement had opened, but, as Musgrave has observed, the bass line accompanying the second theme in Schubert's other late masterpiece in C major, the String Quintet, D. 956 (mm. 46–53).[21] The closing group (beginning in E minor) renews the allusion to Schubert's symphony when, at measure 168, the dotted rhythmic motif from the transition and its associated key of C major suddenly reappear, initiating a spirited back-and-forth exchange between C major and E minor that is settled in favor of the mediant only with the exposition's final cadence (mm. 180–3).

The last allusions to Schubert – again to the quintet as well as the symphony – occur in the coda (mm. 367ff.). Beginning at measure 375, on the heels of a modulation from C minor to E♭ minor, the *marcato* trombone carries the "Bachian" head motif of the main theme through a series of enharmonic modulations that recalls a similar passage in the development of Schubert's symphony (cf. mm. 304ff.). Then, at the Più Allegro (m. 391), Brahms combines a repeated rhythmic idea deriving from the coda of the String Quintet's finale with loud chords in the woodwinds and brass to create one last transformation of the head motif, which is now harmonized by the distinctive chord progression with which the *first* movement of the Quintet begins (I–vii°⁷/V–I). This new combination drives to the glorious apotheosis of the trombone chorale from the slow introduction, whose unexpected return here brings to mind Schubert's stirring recollection of the introductory horn theme in the coda of the "Great" C Major.

Looming even larger in the background of Brahms's work was another symphony in C major, Schumann's Second. Here, no less than in Beethoven's Fifth and Ninth symphonies, was a model, highly respected in its day, of the same plot-archetype of *per aspera ad astra*.[22] Both works show a comparable network of subtle inter-movement thematic references and even similar approaches to the large-scale treatment of tonality; they share, in addition, a number of striking particulars. Consider Schumann's handling of the main subject of his third movement (Adagio, C minor), an expressive theme whose strongly marked succession of intervals, including the highly affective descending diminished fourth, imbues the music with an increasing sense of resignation that finally comes to seem almost overwhelming. As Brahms was perhaps the first to recognize, Schumann alludes here to J. S. Bach's *Musical Offering*, where a very similar idea appears as the main subject of the Largo of the *Sonata sopr'il soggetto reale* (Example 5.2a–b).[23]

Example 5.2: (a) J. S. Bach, *Musical Offering*, Trio sonata, Largo, 1–2; (b) Schumann, Second Symphony, III, 1–4; (c) Schumann, Second Symphony, IV, 63–5

And as Brahms could not have missed, in the finale that follows, this heavily laden "Bachian" melody recurs in a fast tempo and the major mode as the secondary theme of what initially appears to be a lively sonata-rondo movement (Example 5.2c). This implied process is "deformed" in the development, however; working with motifs that are derived from the movement's introductory flourish (mm. 1–4) and the same secondary theme, Schumann gradually reveals a striking "new idea" – an allusion to the beautiful melody from the last song in Beethoven's *An die ferne Geliebte* – that ultimately substitutes for the main theme at the beginning of the recapitulation (mm. 394ff.).

Each of these points is rehearsed in Brahms's sprawling finale (slow introduction and fast movement). Like Schumann, Brahms begins his C minor Adagio with a highly affective melody apparently taken from a movement by Bach (in this instance, as proposed earlier, the chorus "Ach, Herr! lehre uns bedenken") and then later deploys the borrowed idea, suitably transformed in mode and tempo, in an ensuing triumphant Allegro which, like the finale of Schumann's Second, appears at first to be a sonata-rondo. Yet the most striking parallel – and clearest sign of the later composer's "misreading" of his model – may be seen in the process of developing variation that leads to the striking recapitulation of the alphorn theme at measure 285, which far exceeds in length and complexity the

Example 5.3: IV, 1–5; (b) IV, 12–14; (c) IV, 28–31; (d) IV, 61–3; (e) IV, 94–6; (f) IV, 118–19; (g) IV, 185–7; (h) IV, 220–2; (i) IV, 285–8; (j) IV, 301–3

similar process whereby Schumann had evolved the "new theme" that appears at the outset of his recapitulation.

Brahms's process begins in the first measures of the slow introduction, where the head motif of the main theme is adumbrated in the minor mode and over a descending tetrachord (which surely carries its traditional signification of sorrow). Here, of course, the music scarcely reflects the optimistic sentiments of the "Ode to Joy." On the contrary, like the ostinato bass in Bach's *Actus tragicus*, the melody fleshes out the rhetorical figure *saltus duriusculus*, a traditional mourning topos; even the tonality and register of Bach's C minor ostinato eventually are appropriated (see Examples 5.3a–b and compare Example 5.1a).[24] As tension builds over repeated diminished-seventh harmony, a new chromatically inflected version of the descending tetrachord is introduced at measure 28, and when two measures later the

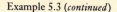

Example 5.3 (*continued*)

dominant is reached, the alphorn theme makes its dramatic first appearance, offering a beautiful major-key transformation of the *saltus duriusculus* figure (compare Examples 5.3a and 5.3c).

This transformation of the prevailing sorrowful ethos, underscored by the appearance of the trombone chorale at measure 47, ensures that when the primary theme of the Allegro is finally introduced (in which, significantly, the head motif and descending tetrachord are superimposed) the major key is guaranteed (Example 5.3d). Then, at precisely the moment in the transitional theme when an echo of the *Freudenthema* is expected, comes instead a clear reference, now in the untroubled major mode, to the distinctive rhythmic profile of Bach's bass line (compare the ending of Example 5.3e with Example 5.1a). The ensuing lively passage eventually leads to the ostinato-based secondary group (beginning in the dominant at m. 118), whose thematic material offers yet another major-key variant of the *saltus durius-culus*, and whose repeated bass line derives from the descending tetrachord that had originally introduced Brahms's melodic version of the figure (compare Example 5.3f with Examples 5.3a and c).[25] Here, of course, the focus naturally falls on the descending tetrachord, and in a remarkable passage that is begun in measure 128 this figure is transposed, chromatically altered (thereby introducing the same augmented second that is found in the original presentation of the head motif), inverted, given new rhythmic shapes, transferred to the upper voices and combined with itself in counterpoint, and, ultimately, developed into a real tune (mm. 132ff.) – which is itself then immediately subjected to a series of transformations (at mm. 136 and 142). After all this, the exposition closes, in E minor, with a new thematic version of motivic material that has not be heard since measures 22–4.

The recapitulatory/developmental passage that follows at measure 186 sets out with a restatement in the tonic of the hymn-like main theme (Example 5.3g). The tune is more richly scored than before, however, and rather than closing as expected in C it is redirected toward the end and settles down instead in E♭, in which key the second strophe is begun (mm. 204ff.). But this statement, too, is soon derailed, first, by a pizzicato passage that brings to mind the troubled slow introduction (compare mm. 208–19 with mm. 6–12 and mm. 16–19) and then by yet another modulation by third, to B major. And if the sudden recurrence in the tonic at measure 220 of the old *animato* transformation of the head motif serves to sweep away those disturbances (Example 5.3h), we none the less find ourselves soon enough back in the midst of development (beginning around m. 232).

Here the material that had originally acted as the bridge is worked out contrapuntally in a passage that recalls a similar episode in the development of the last movement of Mozart's "Jupiter" Symphony (compare mm. 234ff. with mm. 292ff. of Mozart's finale).[26] With the arrival on the dominant of D minor at measure 244 comes a new version of the head motif, set in dialogue between the oboe and flute over a continuation of established scalar patterns in the strings, and soon leading, in measures 246–8, to a subtle "combined reference" to both the alphorn theme (recalled by the descending pattern E–D–C) and head motif (represented by the incomplete neighbor-note pattern C–B♮).[27] The pick-up to measure 268 brings with it yet another version of the head motif, sounding *fortissimo* in the unison wind band, and followed, beginning in measure 274, by a stretta on the opening neighbor-note figure. This quickly builds to a significant new "combined reference" to the alphorn theme and head motif, each now isolated in its own register and played *marcato*. Again the alphorn theme is represented by its initial stepwise descending pattern, which is repeated with much of the same vehemence as in the original build-up occurring in the slow introduction; the neighbor-note figure from the head motif, by contrast, has finally been eliminated here, yielding now to its complement, the falling second (A♭–G).

With the stage thus set for the great climax of the entire symphony, measure 285 ushers in the final transformation of the two original motivic ideas. Remarkably, not only the head motif but the descending tetrachord that has been associated with it from the start both give up their separate identities and take on the shape of the alphorn theme. *Per aspera ad astra*: at first, sounding *fortissimo* in the violins over fierce diminished-seventh harmony, the once reassuring theme seems to have been claimed by the dark sound-world of the opening Adagio. But in a moment that storm passes; as the horn reclaims its theme, the sky clears and brightens once more (Example 5.3i). This is one of the most magical moments in any symphony, and it is only after some exquisite hesitation and stillness – in measures 297–301, the music seems to be experiencing a blissful death – that the animated secondary group steals in to break the spell (Example 5.3j).

What this intricate narrative might mean is suggested by the text of the funeral cantata by Bach from which Brahms seems to have drawn the head motif in the first place, the "germ and root" of which, as Spitta observed, lies in the "contrast … between the wrath of an avenging God and the atoning love of Christ."[28] To be sure, the skeptic Brahms no more would have been able to embrace this précis of Christian salvation history than he would have held with the message contained in Schiller's "Ode to Joy" – at least not literally. But as M. H. Abrams has argued, many Romantics sought to preserve something of the Christian experience by shifting the redemptive goal of the history of humanity from "the reconciliation and reunion with a transcendent God" to forms that were more acceptable to the secular mind and could be located within human experience itself. In this view, as Abrams continues, "the mind of man, whether generic or individual, is represented as disciplined by the suffering which it experiences as it develops through successive stages of decision, conflict, and reconciliation, toward the culminating stage at which, all oppositions having been overcome, it will achieve a full and triumphant awareness of its identity, of the significance of its past, and of its accomplished destiny. The course of human life … is no longer a *Heilsgeschichte* but a *Bildungsgeschichte*; or more precisely, it is a *Heilsgeschichte* translated into the secular mode of a *Bildungsgeschichte*."[29]

It was precisely this kind of "secular Christianity," as Arnold Whittall has noted, that "prompted [Brahms's] non-liturgical but emphatically Biblical German Requiem and gives the Four Serious Songs their unrivalled gravity and sense of strict, human morality" and so, in a more general sense, reflected his world view: "A Bible-reading devotee of Bismarck who had much experience of human weakness (from the onset of Schumann's madness to the breakdown of his parents' marriage), Brahms was clearly more concerned with ways of living life on earth most effectively than with preparing for a possible afterlife."[30] It seems entirely plausible, accordingly, to understand the First Symphony – considered from opening movement to last, across the whole of the finale, or even in the overlapping appearances of the alphorn theme at the culmination of the development – in the same vein, to read it as a *Bildungsgeschichte*, as a playing out of the Christian drama of suffering and redemption in ordinary human experience.

In the foregoing account, much has been made of the roles that are played in the last chapter of this drama by the "Bachian" head motif and alphorn theme, by the eventual triumphant transformation of the one into the other. But how, in this view, do we explain the apotheosis of the trombone chorale that comes in the coda, with all the explicit religious connotations that it leaves as the symphony's final word? This "incongruous" passage, as it were, seems to have troubled Clara Schumann, who wrote: "If I may say something now about the last movement, or, rather, about the very end (Presto), then it is this, that in my opinion, musically speaking, the Presto drops off from the highest inspiration just before. To me, the climax in the Presto lies more in outer than inner motion; the Presto appears not as an outgrowth of the whole, but as a brilliant finish added on."[31] Perhaps, in the end, the returning chorale, completely silent since its brief solemn appearance in the slow introduction but now appearing so brilliantly at the end, does seem out of place; it represents a transcendence that Brahms cannot finally embrace. An early anonymous reviewer in New York sensed as much:

The last movement is not, we find, exactly joyful; it is rather very *intense*; it lacks the spontaneous and simple quality, the *outwardness*, we might say, of joy; and in this respect it strongly and interestingly differs from its prototype of the Ninth symphony. And in this difference we find the keynote of one of Johannes Brahms's chief peculiarities as a composer. He is a modern of the moderns, and this symphony is a remarkable expression of the inner life of this anxious, introverted, over-earnest age, which cannot even be glad in a frank and self-forgetful spirit.[32]

6

Early reception

Hanslick confesses to me that he approaches my symphony with anxiety. Lübke speaks to him too much about late Beethoven, scholarship, and other beautiful things.[1]

I experienced great honor and joy in Baden with Brahms, who was charmingly affable with me and played for me the Tenth Symphony from the page proofs. Yes, yes, yes![2]

I think you are connected with a music lending library? Would you be so kind as to procure for me Brahms's Symphony in orchestra and piano score for a short time on guarantee of the fees required? I'm not learning anything any more of what happens in the world and here you can't get such a thing.[3]

Brahms was not the only composer to introduce a new symphony during the 1876–7 concert season; sharing the circuit with the C Minor that year were fresh symphonic works by Hermann Goetz, Karl Goldmark, Salomon Judasson, Joachim Raff, and Joseph Rheinberger. Yet Brahms's work inevitably drew the most attention. "Seldom, if ever," wrote Eduard Hanslick in December 1876, "has the entire musical world awaited a composer's first symphony with such tense anticipation – testimony that the unusual was expected of Brahms in this supreme and ultimately difficult form."[4] Even before Brahms's career had really taken off, after all, Schumann's "Neue Bahnen" had raised the public's expectations, with its reference to the composer's unknown piano sonatas as "veiled symphonies" and its foretelling of grander works to come. And the long continuing absence of a symphony by Brahms could only be viewed as a puzzling lacuna in the catalogue of an artist who, on the strength of his considerable achievements in the realms of chamber and choral music, had come to be ranked with Wagner. Thus when Brahms finally did speak in a symphonic voice all parties took careful notice.

In an illuminating recent study, Walter Frisch has isolated several themes that figure prominently in the *Rezeptionsgeschichte* of Brahms's symphonic oeuvre. These include what Frisch terms "the Beethoven problem," the notion of "symphony as chamber music" (adumbrated, with a negative slant, by Wagner and later taken up, from varying points of view, by Paul Bekker, Theodor Adorno, and Carl Dahlhaus), the dialectic of "heart vs. brain" (as Schoenberg described the tension between inspiration and intellect), and others that can be grouped under the umbrella – one broad enough to cover Hermann Kretschmar's venerable *Erläuterungen* and Susan McClary's recent narrative readings – of "hermeneutic traditions and the question of program music."[5] Each has surfaced in the present historical and critical study of the C Minor Symphony – in my account of the composer's struggles with the Beethovenian legacy, in the frequent complaints that we have seen were made, even by the composer's intimates, about the work's "cerebral" style, and in the autobiographically inflected *"Manfred* subtext" that I have proposed for the opening movements. But in this final chapter, as we focus on the turbulent early reception of the work, we shall discover that all these topics have a long history.

Some early reactions

Given the length, complexity, and serious demeanor of the C Minor Symphony, Brahms could hardly have been surprised by the lukewarm reaction that it initially sparked. The notices of both the Karlsruhe première, on 4 November 1876, and the performance in Mannheim that was given three days later, to be sure, were decidedly favorable; but the Munich performance that followed on 15 November can only be judged a failure.[6]

Two reviews from this first round of performances merit extensive quotation, since they sound out so clearly a number of leading themes. Consider the incisive comments of Wilhelm Lübke:

Yesterday in the first subscription concert, under Dessoff's direction, we had the first performance of a new large work by Johannes Brahms, his First Symphony (manuscript). It is an orchestral work in the grand style of the late works of Beethoven, whose worthy successor Brahms has here once again proved himself to be. Not really understandable by the layman upon first hearing, this powerful work offers difficulties enough even for the experienced musician. But what can be recognized immediately is the astonishing polyphonic strength of thematic development, the broad truly symphonic design, the richly ordered construction of the whole, the overwhelming power and intensity of the masterly handled orchestra. The first movement especially fascinated through the original strength of its themes and the lively development of the same. The Andante moves in a broad Cantilena and in those spirit-moving, ideal melodies that we find elsewhere in similar impressive power only in Beethoven. With this the lively third movement will captivate the ear and heart most quickly. In the end the last movement builds up, ever swelling, to a majestic, truly heroic height; it sounds at the end like a song of triumph of a noble struggle, which struggles from darkness into light, to rejoicing certainty of victory. The Grand Ducal orchestra, led by Dessoff's sure hand, brought off the difficult task with complete devotion to [making] a beautiful success. The public, which had filled the hall down to the last seat, rewarded the Master with enthusiastic applause. It is a joy, in a time when false prophets are not lacking, to be allowed to accompany a true priest of art step by step through his serious works. Such Brahms has proven himself to be in his *German Requiem*, the *Schicksalslied* of Hölderlein, the *Triumphgesang* [*sic*], and in so many masterpieces of chamber music. We greet with joyful thanksgiving this first symphony of the tireless composer and hope that it will not remain the only one.[7]

Richard Pohl, who witnessed both the Karlsruhe and Mannheim performances, rehearsed many of these same themes of "late Beethoven, scholarship, and other beautiful things"; at the same time, he made reference (what was soon to become *de rigueur*) to the allusion in the finale to the "Ode to Joy," and, in keeping with his *neudeutsche* sympathies, even introduced the intriguing notion that this last movement might embody an extramusical program:

Understandably, the general tension surrounding this work [in the two audiences] was not at all negligible. After being active as a composer for more than twenty years, Brahms has finally come forth with his first symphony. That it must come was for him an artistic necessity; but the longer he hesitated, the more the expectation grew regarding the novelty that he would bring to this greatest of all instrumental forms, the form in which he would express it, and the content [*Gedankeninhalt*] that would be given musical expression.

That this work is significant hardly needs to be asserted after the chamber music that preceded it. Grandly scaled, artfully worked out in the broadest dimensions, unified and rich in mood, always noble in expression, ingenious in its sequence of ideas [*Gedankengang*], tastefully worked out, it brings together all the virtues of Brahms's muse. The basic mood can be described as very dark, almost tragic; the expression builds from the passionate to the powerful and causes us to feel that a distinct, logical sequence of ideas can be found underneath, that poetic content here has attained musical expression. The first three movements can probably be explained without resorting to a program of ideas, but not so the continuous fourth and fifth movements [i.e., the finale]. Here the style is so dramatic in places, the musical language so full of life, that one feels involuntarily led toward a specific meaning, one which, however, only the composer himself would be able to explain with complete certainty. But – he has remained completely silent about it.

These last two movements, however, are also the most significant and arresting; in

81

this symphony, therefore, we perceive an artistic intensification until the end, which raises [the work] to a rank above most of its post-Beethoven sisters ...

From the formal standpoint, Brahms has always made a decided effort not to go beyond the large forms that Beethoven left us, but rather to fill [them] with individual content ... [H]e strives for an intellectual deepening of the content, not for new means of expression. In his symphony, however, he reaches the point at which the inherited forms are unsuitable and insufficient. As strictly as the sonata form of the largely proportioned first movement behaves, as little new as the scherzo offers in this direction, [just] as freely does the composer move in the last two movements, which – in more than one respect – reminds us of the "Ninth," not only in the tragic accents, but even in a melodically related main idea. That Brahms, who has in general followed directly upon Beethoven in a most decisive way, would be sympathetically inclined to do so also in the symphony, could be predicted; but where he will go now in his second symphony, which certainly must come – that is what, after the impression which his First has made on us – we are most expectant to learn.[8]

After these initial tryouts in south-west Germany and Munich came important tests in the musical centers of Vienna and Leipzig. Brahms was warmly welcomed upon his return to the podium in the Imperial City when, on 17 December 1876, he stepped out to lead the orchestra of the Gesellschaft der Musikfreunde. Yet the applause following each of the first three movements lacked conviction, and, though the composer was called back many times at the end, the overall reception was noticeably muted. Several reviewers reminded their readers of Schumann's encomium, and – encouraged by the main theme of the finale – most insisted on measuring the symphony against a Beethovenian yardstick. Some actually charged Brahms with epigonism, while others judged the work too introverted for the Viennese taste, not "popular" enough in tone, inaccessible to all but the connoisseur.[9] Even Hanslick, in an overwhelmingly positive review that left no mistaking his own conviction that his friend had come off well against the Beethovenian standard, complained that Brahms "seems to favour too one-sidedly the great and the serious, the difficult and the complex, and at the expense of sensuous beauty. We would often give the finest contrapuntal device (and they lie bedded away in the symphony by the dozen) for a moment of warm, heart-quickening sunshine."[10]

Leipzig, by contrast, gave Brahms one of his greatest popular triumphs, owing in no small measure to the large contingent of the composer's friends and admirers that helped fill the Gewandhaus for the performance on 18 January 1877. The reaction in the press was far from uniform, however. Hermann Zopff, writing for the "musical left" in the *Neue Zeitschrift*, was rather grudging in his praise of a work that exemplified a genre which, in his view, had largely run its course; from the other side came the comments of Eduard Bernsdorff, an implacably conservative critic for the *Signale für die musikalische Welt*, whose remarks recall Hanslick's gentle reproach about Brahms's overly "brainy" style in downright nasty terms: "The great obstacle to our love for Brahms is that his inventive quality has for us nothing, or too little, that touches the heart and makes one happy; that reflection with him is paramount to inspiration; that he *à tout prix* pushes into the foreground what is interesting at the expense of beauty; and that things farfetched and overstrained in all possible forms and shapes continually claim attention."[11]

Carl Kipke, writing in the *Musikalisches Wochenblatt*, contributed a rather more perceptive (and even-handed) account:

How intimately [Brahms, Schumann, and Beethoven] belong together! In the realm of instrumental music Schumann was Beethoven's most fully entitled heir, and since then Brahms alone has had the power to appropriate so correctly the legacy of both departed ones and to elaborate further toward unique pages ... Next to Beethoven and Schumann, Brahms is probably the most subjective composer of our age; even more than those two Brahms demands of his listener that he completely disregard his own ego [*sein eigenes Ich*], submit himself irresolutely to the composer's own individual process of thought and feeling, and follow the latter in his own self-contemplative examinations with never resting, never loosening self-denial ... The whole composition is without doubt the most significant symphonic accomplishment by far of the post-Schumann–Beethoven era and as such is of undeniable value. In no other similar work of recent times can be seen such a powerful flight of ideas, such a sovereign command of the symphonic style in its highest development. In a word, Brahms's C Minor Symphony, if it is not of precisely the same high birth, may be placed worthily alongside the symphonies of Schumann and Beethoven (with the decided exception of the Ninth). Of the individual movements I might characterize the first, with its wrestling and struggling, as the most significant musically but the second as the most tender. The third movement (Allegretto grazioso), through its almost childlike-naïve manner, is surprisingly soothing after the pathetic tones of the preceding movements. The last movement seems to me to be the weakest of all. Here again, to be sure, the introductory Adagio is a true pearl of musical lyricism, but the succeeding Allegro con brio makes evident an unambiguous incongruity between the aspiration and ability [*Wollen und Können*] of the composer, who does not have the power here to reach the height to which he is evidently striving; only in the coda does he regain the complete power of expression. For all that, as much as I set great store by the extraordinary beauties and the value of Brahms's symphony, I cannot see in it a truly art-advancing accomplishment. This symphony does not open for us a really new perspective on the future; as magnificent and as completely new as its content may in part be, in its essence as a whole it does not go one step beyond the Schumann and first eight Beethoven symphonies.[12]

The equivocation coming at the end – the implication that Brahms had fallen short of expectations, the failure to perceive signs of any genuine artistic "progress" in the symphony – is notable, and, as we shall see, it soon drew Wagner's gleeful assent.

The "Tenth Symphony"

Hans von Bülow's famous aperçu was conceived in the flush of excitement stimulated by his initial experience of the First, when, in September 1877, he met Brahms in Baden and heard there the still-unpublished work performed at the piano. "Brahms was charmingly affable with me," as von Bülow described this encounter to Jessie Laussot in a letter of 25 September, "and played for me the Tenth Symphony from the page proofs. Yes, yes, yes!" A week later, the conductor used the same locution when requesting Brahms's assistance in obtaining proofs of the parts for use in a forthcoming performance in Hannover: "Wouldn't you put in a merciful word to 'Massa' Simrock for the Intendant and Kapellmeister in Welfenheim, so that we can perform the 'Tenth' Symphony in the third subscription concert on the 20th of the month?"[13] And it seems likely that Brahms himself made mention of von Bülow's sobriquet to his friend Adolf Schubring, as we can gather from Schubring's letter to Brahms of 10 October 1877, the very one in which, as we saw in Chapter 5, Schubring had made jest regarding the "double allusion" to Schumann and Beethoven in the main theme of the finale: "It's comical – as I once mentioned to you in Leipzig – that even Beethoven in the last movement of his Ninth (which isn't inferior [in this respect] to the Tenth) joined together Mendelssohn's 'Es ist bestimmt in Gottes Rat' and Papageno's 'Denn alle Vögel sind ja mein.' "[14]

It was not until several weeks later, however, in von Bülow's open letter of 27 October–4 November 1877 to the publisher of the *Signale*, Bartholf Senff, that the provocative expression was introduced to the wider public:

Only since my acquaintance with the Tenth Symphony, *alias* the First Symphony of Brahms, that is, for only six weeks, have I become so intractable toward and hard on Bruch-Stücke and similar compositions [here Bülow is making a pun on the German word *Bruchstück*, meaning fragment, and the popular Second Violin Concerto and other *Stücke* by Max Bruch, which von Bülow found wanting]. I name it the Tenth not as if it were to be ranked after the Ninth; I would place it rather between the Second and the Eroica, just as I maintain that by the First (C major), not the one composed by Beethoven but rather that by Mozart, and known by the name "Jupiter," should be understood. When I furthermore confess that for me, in spite of my partial admiration for Schubert's [symphony], for certain movements in Schumann's (II, 3 and III, 1, 4, etc.), as a complete work of art Mendelssohn's "Scottish" Symphony (No. 3, A minor) occupies first place among the post-Beethoven symphonies, then Herr Professor Joachim, on this ground common to us both, might perhaps be less disinclined to grant to me that Herren Brahms and Bruch have not much more in common with one another than the initial letters [of their names], apart from perhaps equally good musical education ... On the other hand, you do not believe in alliterative rhymes as I do. I am of the opinion that Mozart, Mendelssohn, and Meyerbeer, that Bach, Beethoven, and Brahms do not alliterate with one another without an understanding on the part of chance.[15]

These remarks were rapidly and widely disseminated, and throughout the ensuing concert season, which saw upwards of thirty performances of the newly published symphony, in venues as far-flung as Moscow and Boston, the critical discourse abounded with references, mostly disapproving, to the echoing of von Bülow's claim by the composer's admirers. From an anonymous reviewer of the first performances in New York (December 1877) comes a colorful representation of the conservative position: "How [the work] ever came to be honored with title of 'The Tenth Symphony' is a mystery to us ... The Tenth Symphony! This noisy, ungraceful, confusing and unattractive example of dry pedantry before the masterpieces of Schubert, Schumann, Mendelssohn, Gade, – or even of the reckless and over-fluent Raff! Absurd!"[16] On the other hand, the report by the devoted Wagnerian Wilhelm Tappert on the first Berlin performance, led by Joachim on 11 November 1877, is really no less contemptuous:

The fervor in the hall was frightful, and had it not been a Hochschule concert then the patience of many would probably have given out. At last "the new symphony," the daily gossip in musical circles during the past weeks, began. "That is Beethoven's Tenth!" announced the initiated triumphantly. Missionaries wandered about and tried to convert the heathen. Herr Johannes Brahms ought to bring legal action against everyone who spreads nonsense such as this. Beethoven never wanted to write a Tenth Symphony and if sketches of one were to be found they would have nothing, absolutely nothing in common with Brahms's latest symphonic work. It is a clumsy maneuver once more of the Brahmin caste to produce its "double-B," Beethoven and Brahms, as a slogan and war-cry among the true believers, by which they try to degrade everyone else. Who commands me to think of Beethoven when I hear Brahms? What are the parallels?[17]

For his part, von Bülow had averred that his re-christening of Brahms's symphony was not intended to suggest that the work ought to "be ranked after the Ninth" (although it is difficult to guess what, if anything, he might have meant by placing it instead between Beethoven's Second and Third symphonies). Robert Pascall has proposed that the conductor had wanted only to indicate the inclusion of Brahms's new work as the tenth and latest entry in some "secret list of master-symphonies."[18] That explanation scarcely seems sufficient, however. Von Bülow, formerly allied with Liszt and Wagner in the New German School, understood the musico-political climate of the day as well as anyone, and his reference to the "Tenth Symphony" – which, as we know from Tappert's report, was almost immediately read as "Beethoven's Tenth" – could only have been calculated to incense. Tacitly dismissing Wagner's famous conviction that the choral finale of the Ninth Symphony had at once sounded the death knell of "pure music" and proclaimed the "art of the future" – realized in Wagner's own music drama – von Bülow seems here to be implying that it was Brahms, not the Bayreuth master, who could rightfully claim Beethoven's mantle.

A few short weeks later, in the perceptive notice on the Hamburg performance of 18 January 1878 that was quoted in Chapter 5, Friedrich Chrysander, eschewing any reference to "the Tenth," assessed the historical importance of Brahms's achievement in terms at once more explicit and subtle than von Bülow's:

The symphony by Brahms will soon be evaluated at greater length; for now let us note only that it belongs to those musical works that are significant not only through their specific musical content, but also through the position they occupy in the development of music. The reference to Beethoven, the linkage to the last or Ninth symphony of this master, is so obvious that here, in the case of an artist like Brahms, we must take it, not as a weak and unproductive imitation, but as a conscious intention. And it is precisely this intention, this artistic wish, that lends the work its art-historical significance.

What is involved here is the problem of how to create a counterpart [*Gegenbild*] to the last sections of the Ninth Symphony that would achieve the same effect in nature and intensity without calling on the assistance of song. And insofar as this attempt has succeeded, it signifies an attempt to lead back from the symphony that mixes playing and singing to the purely instrumental symphony. At the same time it signifies an expansion of those effects that can be created through instrumental means alone.[19]

Needless to say, these ideas did not go down well in Bayreuth.

Wagner's Brahms

Wagner himself did not become acquainted with the First until early February 1878, when he acquired copies of the recently published orchestral and piano scores. Cosima preserved her husband's initial reaction in a diary entry of 5–6 February: "The symphony, with all its triviality blown up by orchestral effects, its tremolando theme which might have come from the introduction to a Strauss waltz, we find utterly shocking." Further evidence of Wagner's distaste for the symphony comes from later that year, when, on 22 September, he told Cosima that if he were to write symphonies he would call them " 'symphonic dialogues,' for he would not compose four movements in the old style; but theme and countertheme one must have, and allow them to speak to each other. There is nothing of that kind in the whole of Brahms's symphony."[20]

Yet even as the older composer was grumbling in private, the younger one was being acclaimed in public: during the last week of September Brahms was the guest of honor at the celebration of the fiftieth anniversary of the Hamburg Philharmonic, which included, in addition to a festive banquet and group excursion up the Elbe, three orchestral concerts. Forming the symphonic bill on these occasions were Haydn's Symphony No. 83 in G Minor ("La poule"), Beethoven's "Eroica," the C major Symphony of Schumann, and, in its first performance in his hometown, Brahms's recent Symphony No. 2. As if this symbolic train of masters were not enough, the status which the sudden appearance of two impressive symphonies had brought Brahms as Germany's leading composer of "absolute music" was formally conferred during the following March, when the University of Breslau awarded him an honorary Doctorate of Philosophy. The diploma read: *"vir illustrissimus ... artis musicae severioris in Germania nunc princeps."*

These public acknowledgments, in both word and deed, that Brahms was "Beethoven's heir" was more than Wagner could stand. In July 1879 the older composer, who must have been seething for some time on account of von Bülow's heralding of "the Tenth," vented his anger in the essay "Über das Dichten und Komponieren," writing acidly about the "street-singer" and "Jewish czardas-player" who happened also to be a "sterling symphonist disguised in a Numero Zehn." Though this composer might have been crowned the "serious Prince of Music" (*ernster Musikprinz*), as Wagner punned on the Latin of Brahms's diploma, the face behind his mask – Brahms had been sporting a beard since the previous summer – was perfectly ordinary, which made it all the more unfortunate that "many people [in powerful positions] are actually deceived by the mask, and Hamburg festival banquets and Breslau diplomas perchance come forth as a result."[21]

Wagner continued to dig at Brahms in "Über das Opern-Dichten und Komponieren im Besonderen," which appeared in September 1879.[22] Then, two months later, in "Über die Anwendung der Musik auf das Drama," he mounted a full-scale attack against the "symphony compositions" of Brahms and other composers of the "Romantic–Classical school" by way of validating his own crucial role in history. No longer, to be sure, did he link the birth of music drama directly to the late works of Beethoven; "programmatic instrumental music" now was given its due as a necessary intermediate stage. But, in a vitriolic passage that twists certain locutions found in the more even-handed assessment of Brahms's historical significance by Carl Kipke that was cited above, Wagner held fast to his position that it was only he, not the younger composer, who had truly understood Beethoven's mission and carried out his assignment:[23]

If we take another glance at the "classical" instrumental composition of our most recent times, which has been completely untouched by the aforementioned gestational process [leading to the music drama] [*von dem bezeichneten Gebärungsprozesse unberührt gebliebene "klassisch" Instrumental-Composition*], then we will find that this "classical survivor" ["*klassisch Geblieben*"; i.e., Brahms] is an idle pretense, and beside our great Classical masters has planted us a highly unpleasant hybrid of "wanting to" and "being unable to" [*von Gernwollen und Nichtkönnen*; i.e., the First Symphony].

Programmatic instrumental music, which was viewed by "us" with a timid glance and dubious eye, brought so much novelty in harmonization and theatrical, landscape-painting, and even historical effects, and worked all this out with such moving precision in accordance with an uncommonly virtuosic art of instrumentation, that, in order to continue in the earlier Classical symphony style, what was unfortunately lacking was the real Beethoven, who perchance would have known what to do. We kept silent. When we finally trusted ourselves to open our mouth again symphonically, in order to show what we might yet be able to accomplish, we hit upon nothing else, as soon as we noticed that we were much too tedious and pompous, than decking ourselves out with the fallen feathers of the programmatic oceanic birds [*Sturmvögel*]. The way of our symphonies and the like was and is nowadays *weltschmerzlich* and catastrophic; we are somber and grim, then again dashing and daring; we yearn for the confusion of the dreams of youth; demonic obstacles disturb us; we brood, even rage; and then finally, to *Weltschmerz*, the tooth is pulled out [*wird . . . dem Weltschmerz der Zahn ausgerissen*]; now we laugh and humorously show the gaping gum of the world [*Weltzahnlücke*], competent, sturdy, upright, Hungarian or Scottish, – unfortunately for others boring.

Having made his complicated pun equating the painful process of pulling a tooth (*Zahn*) and the succession of ideas in Brahms's *Numero Zehn* – from the first movement's somber introduction and dashing opening subject through all the brooding and raging that precedes the "grinning" main theme of the finale, with its reference to the "Ode to Joy" – Wagner underscored his point in a less opaque style:

[W]e cannot believe that instrumental music has been assured of a thriving future by the creations of its latest masters. First and foremost, however, we could be doing ourselves some harm by unthinkingly assigning these works to the Beethovenian legacy because we should actually come to realize the completely un-Beethovenian things about them. And that ought not to be too difficult, considering how unlike Beethoven they are in spirit, despite the Beethovenian themes that we still come across.

Later, Wagner returned to the metaphorical toothache, mocking its supposed remedy:

The aforementioned symphony compositions of our newest school – let us call it the Romantic–Classical – are distinguished from the wild beasts of the so-called program music, apart from seeming to us to be wanting of a program, especially by the certain clammy [*zähe*] cast of melody which has been transplanted to them from the "chamber music" that had heretofore been quietly cultivated by their creators. To the "chamber" one had in fact withdrawn. But not, alas, to the beloved little room where Beethoven breathlessly communicated to the few friends who listened in all the Unutterable that he kept for understanding here alone, not there in the spacious concert hall, where he believed it possible to speak in great plastic strokes to the people, to all mankind: in this hallowed "chamber" it had soon grown silent; one then must hear the Master's so-called "last" quartets and sonatas as one played them, namely badly, and at best – not at all, till the way at last was shown by certain outlawed renegades, and one discovered what that chamber music really says. But those [composers of the "Romantic–Classical" school] transferred *their* chamber into the concert hall. What had before been fixed up as quintets and the like was now served up as symphonies. Paltry "melody-chaff" [*Melodien-Häcksel*], comparable to a mixture of hay and old tea, of which no one knows what he is sipping, but dispensed under the label "Genuine" ["*Ächt*"] for the alleged imbibing of *Weltschmerz*.

Here Wagner faulted Brahms for treating the symphony, not, in the manner of Beethoven, as a grand genre directed toward the masses, but as a kind of misplaced chamber music that, presumably, could be appreciated only by the educated élite.[24] To a member of that élite – which in Vienna meant the educated German and Jewish-German liberal-bourgeois Establishment of which Brahms was a part – the same matter took on a different meaning and was cause for a different kind of complaint. Thus these comments from the noted surgeon Theodor Billroth, an accomplished musical amateur and one of the composer's closest friends, who shared them with Brahms following a rehearsal of the very piece that Wagner had found so irritating:

I wished I could hear the [C Minor] symphony all by myself, in the dark, and began to understand King Ludwig's private concerts [*Sonderabenden*]. All the silly, everyday people who surround you in the concert hall and of whom in the best case [only] fifty have enough intellect and artistic feeling to grasp the essence of such a work at the first hearing – not to speak of understanding; all that upsets me in advance. I hope, however, that the musical masses here have enough musical instinct to understand that something great is happening there in the orchestra.[25]

Certainly Brahms never pandered to the "musical masses." He worked during a time that saw the establishment of what J. Peter Burkholder has termed the "concert hall museum"; and, in that light, a good case can be made that Brahms determined to hold fast to his "difficult" style because he was writing less for his own contemporaries than for a posterity that would be able to rehear and study his works closely – and would judge them against a "permanent collection" of masterpieces. As Burkholder notes, Brahms's success in securing his place in the canon rested to a large degree upon his ability – deriving from his practice of allusion-making, through which he was able to state his pedigree in a distinctive voice – to resolve the related oppositions of "the new with the old" and "of emulation and originality." But Brahms's canonization was owing in no less measure to his ability to negotiate a third dialectic, "between the present and the future – the requirement that a work demonstrate lasting value, rewarding frequent rehearings and becoming more loved as it becomes more familiar, and yet at the same time have enough immediate appeal to move the listener to seek out a second hearing."[26] Therein, it would seem, lies one key to understanding the differing fates of a Goetz or Rheinberger and Brahms. Which brings us back, finally, to von Bülow, testifying in August 1888 to the speed with which the latter found an honored place in the museum:

Through absorption in Brahms – who of course wrote no "Beethoven's Tenth Symphony" nor, unfortunately, the finale of the Ninth, which he – potentiâ – would have been able to do to the greater glory of the first three movements – the old Olympus of Bach, Handel, Mozart, Haydn, *et al.*, has become understandable to me for the first time, to be worshipped in its appropriateness, spirit, and truth, to the liberation of the heart and brain.[27]

Appendix

Max Kalbeck's "program" for the First Symphony, first published in *Deutsche Rundschau* 92 (July–September 1897), 87–8:

Brahms' erste Sinfonie.

Prometheus.

(1876.)

Erster Satz:

Horch auf! ein Ahnen, fernher, grollend, ruft mich wach.
Das ist Dein Sang, Prometheus! Erst wie durchs Hochgebirg'
Riß mich's dahin, durch Schlucht und Abgrund, bahnenlos.
Nebel und Nacht! und in Wolken die Gipfel! Ein Donnern rollt
Die Wände nieder. Heiße Bäche zügellos
Klingen darein. Die wirbelnde Windsbraut segt die Bahn.
Die Dryade seufzt. In den Lüften hangt ein Weheschrei,
und der Geier kreischt: denn hier, hier grollt der Gefesselte!

Zweiter Satz:

Weicht nicht die Wolke? Friedlich, dehnet ein Anger sich,
Wo alles Duft, und der Wind träumt, und mit der Sonne spielt
Der Schatten der Rose; es wandelt die Taube am Rankt des Sees.
Da sammelten sich die Weiber der Tiefe mit feuchtem Haar
Und schau'n hinauf meertiefen Blicks, die freundlichen
Ozeaniden, und stimmten süßesten Wehesang:
"Der Edle leidet! Weinet, ihr Unsterblichen!"
Unsterbliches Weinen! Hörst Du es, einsam Grollender?

Dritter Satz:

Der Geier floh. So fliehet der Tag. Und aus Busch und Wald
Hüpft zärtlich der Schwarm der blühenden, ewig jungen Luft,
Die Nymphen, die blumenstreuenden, übend gewohnten Tanz.
Denn sie lernten nur ihn und lerneten die Thräne nicht.

Nun schreiten sie zart behende, ein melancholischer,
Traumhaft verschlungner, dämmerungtrunkner Reigentanz,
Daß lächelnd es seh'n die Klagemüden. Zuckte nicht
Um die Lippe ein Lächeln Dir selbst, einsam Grollender?
                    Vierter Satz:
    Und das All will nachten, ruhend in Andächtigkeit.
Er lauscht. Nur Er, der ewig einsam Wachende –
An den Himmel den Scheitel lehnt er und athmet tief und schwer,
Daß des Busens dreimal eisengeschlagene Fesseln klirr'n,
Und ein Dröhnen reißt durch das Erdrund. Und er betet stolz:
Mein ist der Sieg. An meiner Seele fraß der Schmerz,
Der Sturm zerschlug den Leib mir und der Blitz mein Haupt,
Und jeden Morgen kehren alte Qualen neu!
Ich aber steh' und fühle dieses Leibes Kraft
Und bebe nur vor dieses Herzens heil'ger Gluth
Und juble Deinen großen Thaten, Gott in mir,
Der aus dem Schmerz mir schenkte die Unsterblichkeit.
Die Zeit ist ewig, aber Du bist ewiger! –
Der Abgrund hört es, und die Sphären tönen nach:
Der Sieg ist sein, des an die Qual Geschmiedeten!

                                    Beatus Rhenanus (Max Kalbeck)

Brahms's First Symphony

Prometheus

(1876)

First movement

Listen up! A premonition, rumbling from the distance, calls me from slumber. That is
your song Prometheus! It tore me to itself, just as though through mountains high,
through glen and over abyss, pathless. Fog and night! Peaks in clouds! Thunder rolls
down the mountainsides. Unbridled, searing torrents resound about. The tornado's
bride sweeps clear the path. Lone dryad sighs. In the breezes there lingers a cry of
woe, and the vulture screeches: For here, here is the bound man who groans!

Second movement

Will the cloud not disperse? A rolling landscape expands peacefully, the shadow of the
rose plays with the sun, the wind dreams and everywhere a fragrance; a dove courses
on the edge of the lake. With damp locks the feminine forms of the deep gathered and
gaze upward with sea-depth view, the friendly Oceanides, now joined in the sweetest

of lamentation: "The noble man suffers! Wail, you immortals!" Immortal wailing. Do you hear it, lonely moaner?

Third movement

The vulture fled. Thus flees the day. And from thicket and forest tenderly slips the swarm of the blooming, ever-youthful aeries, the nymphs, strewing blossoms, practicing the accustomed dance. That alone they have learned and learned tears not at all. Their tenderly nimbling steps glide them in a round dance, melancholic, engulfed by dream, and by twilight transfixed, so that the lament-weary see it, smiling. Did not a smile twitch about your lips as well, lonely moaner?

Fourth movement

And the universe wills night, resting in meditation. He listens. He alone, the ever-lonely wakeful man – he leans his crown to heaven and breathes deeply, heavily, so that the thrice forged chains of his breast rattle and a quake roars through the earth. And proudly he gives thanks: Mine is the victory. Pain ate at my soul, tempest tore my body asunder and lightning my head, and each morning old pains return anew! But I hold firm and feel the power of this body, and tremble only before the sacred ardour of this heart and rejoice in thy grand deeds, god within me, for from my pain you have given the gift of immortality. Time is eternal, but Thou art more eternal! – The abyss hears this and the spheres resound in echo: the victory is his, the one who has been forged to agony!

Translated by Alan H. Krueck

Notes

1 Frustrated efforts

1 Quoted in Eduard Crass, *Johannes Brahms* (Leipzig, 1957), 36.

2 The première was given in Karlsruhe on 4 November 1876 and was followed by performances in Mannheim (7 November 1876), Munich (15 November 1876), Vienna (17 December 1876), Leipzig (18 January 1877), Breslau (23 January 1877), Cambridge (7 March 1877), and London (31 March and 16 April 1877); Brahms conducted every performance except for those in Karlsruhe (Otto Dessoff), Cambridge (Joseph Joachim), and London (Augustus Manns and William Cusins).

3 The complete tripartite holograph is found in the Pierpont Morgan Library, New York (Mary Flagler Cary Music Collection), and has been published in facsimile as Johannes Brahms, *Symphony No. 1 in C Minor, Op. 68: The Autograph Score*, ed. Margit L. McCorkle (New York, 1986). The middle movements of this score were used as the engraver's models for the first edition (N. Simrock, 1877). The engraver's models for the outer movements, copyist's manuscripts that were missing for several decades, recently came to light and have been acquired by the Brahms-Institut an der Musikhochschule Lübeck (Sammlung Hofmann). Although it cannot be determined when the copy of the first movement was made, the copy of the fourth movement can be dated to late November 1876, between the time of the first performances in Munich and Vienna; see *Johannes Brahms Briefwechsel* (hereafter *Briefwechsel*), 19 vols. to date (consisting of 16 orig. vols., rev. edns [Berlin, 1912–22; repr. Tutzing, 1974] and a *Neue Folge* consisting of 3 vols. to date [Tutzing, 1991–]), vol. XVI: *Johannes Brahms im Briefwechsel mit Otto Dessoff*, ed. Carl Krebs (1922), 150. The only other extant primary sources are both related to a preliminary version of the slow movement. A sketch for this music is preserved in the Pierpont Morgan Library (on loan from Robert Owen Lehman); a handful of string parts that were used in the first few performances are owned by the Gesellschaft der Musikfreunde, Vienna.

4 *Neue Zeitschrift für Musik* 20 (1853), 185–6. Clara Schumann's detailed diary entry for October 1853 recalls both the tone and substance of "Neue Bahnen" and records a similar prophecy: "A beautiful future is in store for him, for when he writes for orchestra for the first time, only then will he have found the proper field for his fantasy!" See Berthold Litzmann, *Clara Schumann: Ein Künstlerleben nach Tagebüchern und Briefen*, 3 vols. (Leipzig, 1902–8), II, 281. Unless otherwise noted, all translations are my own.

5 *Robert Schumanns Briefe, Neue Folge*, ed. F. Gustav Jansen (Leipzig, 1904), 390. The hope never faded during Schumann's last few remaining years. To his wife, Clara, he noted on 6 January 1855: "A symphony or opera that makes an enthusiastic effect and great sensation is the fastest way to promote all the other compositions, too. He must" (*ibid.*, 404). A message to Joachim written on 10 March 1855 recalls the imagery of "Neue Bahnen" even more closely: "If only now he ... were to step up to the masses, the choir and orchestra. That would be magnificent" (*ibid.*, 405).

6 Quoted in Max Kalbeck, *Johannes Brahms*, rev. edns, 4 vols. in 8 (Berlin, 1915–21; repr. Tutzing, 1976), I, 166.

7 The relation between the first movements of the sonata and concerto is reported by Brahms's friend Albert Dietrich; see his *Erinnerungen an Johannes Brahms in Briefen besonders aus seiner Jugendzeit* (Leipzig, 1898), 45, republished as *Erinnerungen an Johannes Brahms in Briefen aus seiner Jugendzeit* (Leipzig, 1989), 151. The earliest mention of the sonata appears in a letter from Julius Otto Grimm to Joseph Joachim; see *Briefwechsel*, vols. V–VI: *Johannes Brahms im Briefwechsel mit Joseph Joachim*, ed. Andreas Moser, 2 vols. (vol. 1: 3rd rev. edn, 1921; vol. 2: 2nd rev. edn, 1912), V, 31. Moser cites the date of this document as 9 March, but this cannot be correct; the letter includes a report on the trip to Cologne that Grimm and Brahms made together at the end of that month in order to attend a performance of the Ninth as well as a reference to a certain pair of letters from Brahms to Joachim that can be identified as being those of 1 April and 7 April (*Briefwechsel*, V, 34–9). The correct date of the letter probably is 9 April 1854, as given in Kalbeck, *Brahms*, I, 166. There is, however, no reason to hold with Kalbeck's view that Brahms began to compose the piece only after hearing the Cologne performance of the Ninth and thus produced the first three movements in less than two weeks' time. Much more likely is it that Brahms worked on the piece throughout the entire difficult month following Schumann's suicide attempt, which he spent in the Schumann home in Düsseldorf, where he would have had access to scores of both Beethoven's and Schumann's symphonies.

8 *Briefwechsel*, V, 46–7. Clara Schumann noted the rehearsals in her diary entries for 24 and 28 May 1854; see Litzmann, *Clara Schumann*, II, 316–18.

9 *Briefwechsel*, V, 55–6; see also *Briefwechsel*, vol. IV: *Johannes Brahms im Briefwechsel mit J. O. Grimm*, ed. Richard Barth (1912), 13.

10 Robert Schumann, *Gesammelte Schriften über Musik und Musiker*, 5th edn, 2 vols., ed. Martin Kreisig (Leipzig, 1914), I, 329; *Clara Schumann–Johannes Brahms: Briefe aus den Jahren 1853–1896*, ed. Berthold Litzmann, 2 vols. (Leipzig, 1927), I, 139. For a somewhat different reading of the evidence, see George S. Bozarth, "Brahms's First Piano Concerto op. 15: Genesis and Meaning," in *Beiträge zur Geschichte des Konzerts: Festschrift Siegfried Kross zum 60. Geburtstag*, ed. Reinmar Emans and Matthias Wendt (Bonn, 1990), 211–23.

11 *Schumann–Brahms Briefe*, I, 69; Christopher Reynolds, "A Choral Symphony by Brahms?" *19th-Century Music* 9 (1985/86), 3–25.

12 *Schumann–Brahms Briefe*, I, 76. Work on the concerto movement dates principally from the fall of 1856. The symphony's scherzo, on the other hand, was revived only much later, in the funeral march of the *German Requiem*; see Dietrich, *Erinnerungen an Johannes Brahms*, 45 (new edition, p. 151). For a speculative account of the eventual fate of other parts of the abandoned symphony, see Reynolds, "A Choral Symphony by Brahms?" 14–18.

13 *Neue Zeitschrift für Musik* 50 (1859), 272.

14 Thus these remarks to Joachim: "[Liszt's] compositions are becoming worse and worse, e.g., Dante!"; and "Otten was recently the first here [in Hamburg] who brought Liszt into a respectable (would-be respectable) concert ... I expect a symphonic poem from him shortly and fear the plague is spreading wider and the ass's ears of the public will grow even longer." *Briefwechsel*, V, 248–9, 258–9.

15 For a compendium of Brahms's allusions, see James Webster, "Schubert's Sonata Form and Brahms's First Maturity (II)," *19th-Century Music* 3 (1979/80), 59–60, and the references cited there.

16 Renate Hofmann, "Johannes Brahms im Spiegel der Korrespondenz Clara Schumanns," in *Brahms und seine Zeit: Symposion Hamburg 1983*, ed. Constantin Floros, Hans Joachim Marx, and Peter Petersen (Laaber, 1984), p. 51; *Briefwechsel*, V, 215; Litzmann, *Clara Schumann*, III, 47–8. On the two scherzi, see *Briefwechsel*, IV, 77; and *Briefwechsel*, V, 228–30. On the preparations for the Hamburg performance, see *Briefwechsel*, V, 198–9, 235; it is clear from the context that these two undated letters, entered as nos. 142 and

170 in the third edition of the correspondence, belong together and date from February 1859.

17 *Briefwechsel*, V, 226–7. It is clear from the context that this letter (no. 163 in the third edition) should follow no. 185 and thus dates from December 1859, not, as suggested by Moser, December 1858. See also Clara's letter to Brahms of 21 December 1859: "Hopefully you received the music paper in time? And are trumpets and drums already shining on it resplendently?" (*Schumann–Brahms Briefe*, I, 291).

18 Kalbeck, *Brahms*, I, 339. Brahms's last remark is corrected in accordance with Bargheer's "Erinnerungen an Johannes Brahms in Detmold 1857–1865" (unpublished typescript preserved in the Lippische Landesbibliothek, Detmold), from which Kalbeck derived his account.

19 *Briefwechsel*, V, 256, 260, 258, 261. The emphasis on the word "Serenade," which is not included in the published edition, is found in the original letter, preserved in Hamburg, Staats- und Universitätsbibliothek Carl von Ossietzky.

20 Dietrich, *Erinnerungen an Brahms*, 42 (new edition, p. 141); and "Fragebogen für Herrn Hofkapellmeister Albert Dietrich," ed. Max Kalbeck, transcribed in Musikantiquariat Hans Schneider, *Katalog 100. Johannes Brahms: Leben und Werk, seine Freunde und seine Zeit* (Tutzing, 1964), 15–16 (emphasis added and inaccurate transcription of "D-moll" in place of "C-moll" corrected).

21 Kalbeck, *Brahms*, I, 233, and III, 93.

22 "For inner reasons we have dated the beginnings, or, as we prefer to say, the germ of the C-minor Symphony to the year 1855" (Kalbeck, *Brahms*, III, 92).

23 *Briefwechsel*, V, 262–3, 263–4, 266–7. See also Joachim's letter to Clara Schumann of *c.* 13 March 1860, in *Letters from and to Joseph Joachim*, trans. Nora Bickley (London, 1914), 193–4.

24 *Briefwechsel*, V, 270–1. Clara's letter to Joachim reads: "Do not be alarmed at the fearful letter enclosed, but read it and then advise me. I cannot go there to celebrate a festival like that with people whom (as a musician) I despise from the bottom of my soul. Shall I say just what I feel about it? How these Weimar folk do intrude whenever it is a question of boasting of Robert's friendship!" Letter of 25 April 1860, in *Letters from and to Joachim*, 199–200.

25 *Neue Zeitschrift für Musik* 52 (25 May 1860), 200.

26 *Neue Zeitschrift für Musik* 52 (4 May 1860), 169–70; *Berliner Musik-Zeitung Echo* 10 (6 May 1860), 142; translations of both texts are given in David Brodbeck, "Brahms, the Third Symphony, and the New German School," in *Brahms and His World*, ed. Walter Frisch (Princeton, 1990), 79–80.

27 *Briefwechsel*, V, 282–3, 284.

28 The unauthorized publication of the "Manifesto" seems at first only to have strengthened the determination of the young composers to proceed in their attack. On 27 May 1860 Ferdinand Hiller noted in his diary that he had met with Brahms, Joachim, Scholz, Robert Radeke, and other musicians in Düsseldorf and had discussed their "Declaration of War against Brendel's Newspaper," about which he said, "I oppose it." See *Aus Ferdinand Hillers Briefwechsel: Beiträge zu einer Biographie Ferdinand Hillers*, ed. Reinhold Sietz, 7 vols. (Cologne, 1958–70), I (1958), 161. Scholz later recalled that Hiller had advised the group that "the best means of struggle would be to create good music"; see Bernhard Scholz, *Verklungene Weisen* (Mainz, 1911), 142. Hiller's counsel evidently prevailed, as the subject thereafter disappeared from the Brahms–Joachim correspondence.

29 *Neue Zeitschrift für Musik* 52 (15 June 1860), 224.

30 *Briefwechsel*, V, 285; *Schumann–Brahms Briefe*, I, 312 (emphasis added).

31 Robert Fink, "Desire, Repression & Brahms's First Symphony," *repercussions* 2 (1993), 79–81.

32 *Neue Zeitschrift für Musik* 51 (5 August 1859), 48–9. This review is found in Pohl's lengthy report on Brendel's *Tonkünstlerversammlung*, carried over several issues in the summer of

1859. In the same series is found an essay on the history of harmony by C. F. Weitzmann, which Brahms ridiculed in a letter to Joachim of August 1859.

33 Significantly, it was at precisely this time that Adolf Schubring began in the *Neue Zeitschrift* his lengthy series of "Schumanniana," which championed Brahms and a handful of other composers of "the center," not those of "the musical left," as the true followers of the late composer; see Walter Frisch, "Brahms and Schubring: Musical Criticism and Musical Politics at Mid-Century," *19th-Century Music* 7 (1983/84), 271–81.

34 Litzmann, *Clara Schumann*, III, 123.

35 Dietrich published this letter with the erroneous date of "early January [18]63" (see *Erinnerungen an Brahms*, 46; new edition, p. 153); my translation is from Styra Avins, *Letters from the Life of Johannes Brahms* (Oxford, in preparation), where it is correctly assigned to early September.

36 *Briefwechsel*, V, 320, 321.

37 Letter of 22 July 1864, in *Schumann–Brahms Briefe*, I, 461.

38 Raymond Knapp, "Brahms and the Problem of the Symphony: Romantic Image, Generic Conception, and Compositional Challenge" (Ph.D. dissertation, Duke University, 1987), 2 vols., I, 20–1.

39 *Schumann–Brahms Briefe*, I, 433–4, 438; *Briefwechsel*, vol. VII: *Johannes Brahms im Briefwechsel mit Hermann Levi, Friedrich Gernsheim sowie den Familien Hecht und Fellinger*, ed. Leopold Schmidt (1910), 15, 20; unpublished letters from Schubring to Brahms of 14 September 1866 and 9 February 1869 (Hamburg, Staats- und Universitätsbibliothek, Brahms-Archiv [Signatur 1965.2201]); *Briefwechsel*, vol. XVIII: *Johannes Brahms im Briefwechsel mit Julius Stockhausen*, ed. Renate Hofmann (1993), 36; and Dietrich, *Erinnerungen an Brahms*, 60; new edition, p. 195 (translated and correctly dated in Florence May, *The Life of Johannes Brahms*, 2 vols. [London, 1905], II, 50).

40 *Briefwechsel*, VII, 62.

41 *Briefwechsel*, vol. III: *Johannes Brahms im Briefwechsel mit Karl Reinthaler, Max Bruch, Hermann Deiters, Friedr. Heimsoeth, Karl Reinecke, Ernst Rudorff, Bernhard und Luise Scholz*, 2nd. edn. ed. Wilhelm Altmann (1912), 101, 103–4.

42 Quoted in Christopher Fifield, *Max Bruch: His Life and Works* (London, 1988), 79–80. This passage is remarkably reminiscent of Schumann's letter to Joachim of 6 January 1854 (see note 5).

43 Letter of 21 January 1867, quoted in Wilhelm Lauth, *Max Bruchs Instrumentalmusik* (Cologne, 1967), 10 (emphasis in the original).

44 Quoted in Wilhelm Lauth, "Entstehung und Geschichte des ersten Violinkonzertes Op. 26 von Max Bruch," in *Max Bruch-Studien*, ed. Dietrich Kämper (Cologne, 1970), 62.

45 Quoted in Lauth, *Bruchs Instrumentalmusik*, 38; *idem*, "Entstehung und Geschichte des ersten Violinkonzertes," 63.

46 Quoted in Lauth, "Entstehung und Geschichte des ersten Violinkonzertes," 63–4 (emphasis in the original).

47 *Aus Ferdinand Hillers Briefwechsel*, I, 115.

48 *Briefwechsel*, III, 92–3. See also Clara Schumann's report to Brahms in a letter of 5 February 1870 that Bruch had recently spoken to her about the *Alto Rhapsody* in a manner that was "so ingenious and so warm that it put [her] in quite a mellow mood" (*Schumann–Brahms Briefe*, I, 612); Bruch subsequently praised the *Rhapsody* and several of Brahms's other recent vocal works in his own letter to the composer of 6 May 1870 (*Briefwechsel*, III, 99–100). Levi, on the other hand, continued to get his digs in concerning Bruch's abilities as an instrumental composer; on 22 March 1869 the conductor reported to Brahms that "yesterday I played Bruch's symphony and in so doing received confirmation that my silence when he played it to us in Cologne had been eloquent and justified" (*Briefwechsel*, VII, 36). And, if we are to believe Ernst Rudorff's recollection regarding a Berlin performance of the D Major Serenade in November of that year, Bruch had not been entirely won over to Brahms's cause (see Ernst

Rudorff, "Johannes Brahms: Erinnerungen und Betrachtungen," *Schweizerische Musikzeitung* 97 [1957], 81).

49 *Briefwechsel*, III, 97–8. For Brahms's acknowledgment of the dedication, see *ibid.*, 92. Bruch's concern about the details of performances can be seen in his letter to Brahms of 25 February 1869, in which he gave minute accounts of several recent performances of the *German Requiem* (*ibid.*, 95–6).

50 *Briefwechsel*, IX, 95. Brahms's skepticism regarding his more "industrious" colleagues was probably fueled also by his friend Dietrich, who had recently honored him with the dedication of a Symphony in D Minor, Op. 20. Although Brahms acknowledged this honor in letters to Dietrich from the fall of 1869 ("the dedication of your symphony gave me the greatest joy") and February 1870 ("I've withheld already too long my thanks for your symphony. You've delighted me heartily with the beautiful present and it would be even more beautiful if an orchestra were to bring it to life"), earlier, in a letter to Clara Schumann of October 1868, he had let on with his true feelings about the piece: "A symphony by Dietrich will played for you in Oldenburg. It would be better if you used a little more gentleness than frankness there!" See Dietrich, *Erinnerungen an Brahms*, 66, 66–7 (new edition, pp. 215, 217); *Schumann–Brahms Briefe*, I, 601.

51 *Pace* Tovey, who believed that the composer "kept the first three movements with him for ten years before attacking the finale" (Donald Francis Tovey, *Essays in Musical Analysis*, vol. I: *Symphonies* [London, 1948], 84; see also Knapp's comments about the genesis of the piece in "Brahms and the Problem of the Symphony," I, 73–4). As Daniel Beller-McKenna has observed (private communication), the text of the alphorn theme alludes to the first stanza of the poem by Eichendorff that Brahms had set as the third of the Four Songs, Op. 17, for women's choir, two horns, and harp (1860): "Wohin ich geh und schaue, in Feld und Wald und Tal, vom Berg hinab in die Aue, viel schöne, hohe Fraue, grüss ich dich tausendmal."

52 Quoted in Kalbeck, *Brahms*, I, 165.

2 Completion, first performances, and publication

1 Letter from the fall of 1876 to Carl Reinecke (*Briefwechsel*, III, 141). Similar locutions are found in letters of October 1876 to Ernst Frank: "[T]he symphony is long and difficult" (Alfred Einstein, "Briefe von Brahms an Ernst Frank," *Zeitschrift für Musikwissenschaft* 4 [1921/22], 394); Franz Wüllner: "My symphony is long and in C minor" (*Briefwechsel*, vol. XV: *Johannes Brahms im Briefwechsel mit Franz Wüllner*, ed. Ernst Wolff [1922], 69); and Johann Herbeck: "My symphony is long and hardly charming" (quoted in Ingrid Fuchs, "Zeitgenössische Aufführungen der ersten Symphonie Op. 68 von Johannes Brahms in Wien: Studien zur Wiener Brahms-Rezeption,"*Brahms-Kongress Wien 1983, Kongressbericht*, ed. Susanne Antonicek and Otto Biba [Tutzing, 1988], 170).

2 Thus Wagner's spiteful remarks about Brahms in the essay "On Conducting" (1869); see "Über das Dirigiren," in Richard Wagner, *Gesammelte Schriften und Dichtungen*, 3rd edn, 10 vols. (Leipzig, 1887–8), vol. VIII (1888), 261–337.

3 *Johannes Brahms und Fritz Simrock. Weg einer Freundschaft: Briefe des Verlegers an den Komponisten*, ed. Kurt Stephenson (Hamburg, 1961), 50; see also 46 and 57.

4 *Briefwechsel*, IX, 92. See also Brahms's letter to Simrock of 23 October 1871: "Bruch had written to me about a Third Symphony. Therefore, take up your pestering [for a symphony] with him. [*Also richten Sie Ihre Tretmühle auf ihn.*] My phlegm and laziness have not been altered by it" (*ibid.*, 100).

5 See *Briefwechsel*, vol. XIV: *Johannes Brahms im Briefwechsel mit Breitkopf & Härtel, Bartholf Senff, J. Rieter-Biedermann, E. W. Fritzsch und Robert Lienau*, ed. Wilhelm Altmann (1920), 183–4; Karl Geiringer, *Brahms: His Life and Works*, 3rd edn, enl. and rev. (New York, 1982), 103–4; *Aus Hillers Briefwechsel*, II, 129; and *Briefwechsel*, III, 30, 156–8, 119, and 101–4;

Briefwechsel, XVI: *Johannes Brahms im Briefwechsel mit Philipp Spitta*, ed. Carl Krebs (1920), 41–5.

6 See Otto Biba, "Brahms und die Gesellschaft der Musikfreunde in Wien," in *Brahms-Kongress Wien 1983*, 45–65. See also Brahms's oblique reference to the Gesellschaft position in his letter to Clara Schumann of 28 March 1870 (*Schumann–Brahms Briefe*, I, 617), as well as his discussions with Levi concerning the post (*Briefwechsel*, VII, 63–5, 83–90 *passim*).

7 *Briefwechsel*, VI, 76.

8 *Briefwechsel*, XVI, 60; the correspondence relevant to the entire episode is found in *ibid.*, 46–61.

9 Kalbeck, *Brahms*, III, 89–90. Brahms even permitted himself to mention the piece to the eager Simrock when the two met in July; see *Briefwechsel*, IX, 181, 187.

10 *Briefwechsel*, IX, 187; *Briefwechsel*, XV, 59.

11 George Henschel, *Personal Recollections of Johannes Brahms* (Boston, 1907), 39; see also Kalbeck, *Brahms*, III, 82–3.

12 Brahms must have concluded all significant work on the first movement, including the addition of the belatedly conceived slow introduction, at some earlier date; as we shall see, he carried with him to Lichtental a set of parts for the opening Allegro. Whether these parts had actually been used in a private trial performance, perhaps with the Gesellschaft orchestra, remains an intriguing but open question.

13 Litzmann, *Clara Schumann*, III, 339–40. The diary entry gives no indication that Clara recalled having played the first movement fourteen years earlier or having received the alphorn theme in the summer of 1868.

14 *Briefwechsel*, XVI, 141. Simrock must have learned about Brahms's work of the summer from Henschel, whom he met in August. Twice the publisher inquired about the work, the second time, in a letter of 30 September, pressing Brahms for his "Cliffs of Wissow Symphony" (*Wissower Klinken-Sinfonie*), alluding to the famous chalk cliffs on Rügen (*Brahms und Simrock*, 84). On 5 October, to Simrock's great joy, Brahms confirmed the report: "A beautiful symphony is stuck on the cliffs of Wissow. I believe Henschel has made a song about it, E♭ major, ⁴ time [i.e., "Wo Engel hausen"], just ask for it" (*Briefwechsel*, X, 13). Two weeks later, in a letter to Joachim, the composer used the same colorful description of the work, which "unfortunately is not the beautiful new 'To the Cliffs of Wissow,' but rather an old acquaintance in that famous C minor" (*Briefwechsel*, VI, 129).

15 *Briefwechsel*, XVI, 142–3.

16 *Briefwechsel*, XVI, 144. Although this letter (no. 26 in Krebs's edition) carries no date or postmark, it can be dated 12 October on the basis of the postmark that is found on the card that Brahms sent to Dessoff later on the same day (which is erroneously entered as no. 25 in Krebs's edition): "I forgot to put rehearsal letters in the score. Would you be so friendly as to finish that – and not too few, which is my mistake" (*ibid.*, 143).

17 Einstein, "Briefe von Brahms an Ernst Frank," 392; *Briefwechsel*, XV, 67; Johannes Brahms, *Mit den Gedanken in Wien: 5 Briefe*, ed. Otto Biba, trans. Eugene Hartzell (Vienna, 1984), 10 (German original), 22 (translation).

18 Einstein, "Briefe von Brahms an Ernst Frank," 392–4; *Briefwechsel*, XV, 68; *Johannes Brahms in Wien. Ausstellung. Archiv der Gesellschaft der Musikfreunde in Wien*, ed. Otto Biba (Vienna, 1983), 51. Around the same time Brahms received an inquiry about the piece from a representative of the Gewandhaus concerts in Leipzig. The composer's response was directed to Carl Reinecke, conductor of the Gewandhaus Orchestra, with whom he eventually arranged a performance for 18 January 1877; see *Briefwechsel*, III, 139–41.

19 Otto Billroth, *Billroth und Brahms im Briefwechsel* (Berlin and Vienna, 1935), 222–3 (translation after Avins, *Letters from the Life of Brahms*).

20 Quoted in Otto Biba, "Brahms, Wagner und Parteiungen in Wien," *Musica* 37 (1983), 21.

21 Ingrid Fuchs has suggested instead that Brahms might have been motivated by a "guilty conscience" regarding the circumstances of his resignation as Concert Director of the

Gesellschaft der Musikfreunde in the previous year and by a desire to head off any rumors concerning this episode ("Zeitgenössische Aufführungen der ersten Symphonie," 169–70).

22 *Briefwechsel*, XVI, 144–5. This letter includes a postscript: "Your card just came. I entered the rehearsal letters at 7:00 this morning. They go up to Q; hopefully that will be enough." An explanation for Dessoff's jest about Kleinmichel can be found in the pages of the *Signale für die musikalische Welt*, where it was reported that "the treasured pianist and composer Herr Richard Kleinmichel is presently in the midst of a longer stay in Leipzig. He has brought along a recently completed symphony, whose first performance he has in mind to give here" (*Signale für die musikalische Welt* 34 [October 1876], 936).

23 Both letters are found in *Briefwechsel*, XVI, 146; the second is signed "Ihr Jesuwiter."

24 *Briefwechsel*, XVI, 147. Dessoff's remark about the first four measures of the Adagio suggest that he immediately recognized Brahms's allusions therein to Beethoven's C Minor Piano Concerto, Op. 37; see below, Chapter 4.

25 *Briefwechsel*, XVI, 148. Although Dessoff had already received parts for the first movement, it was only now, following the confirmation of the performance, that Brahms needed to send him the full score.

26 *Schumann–Brahms Briefe*, II, 93–4. That this tempo change, along with an inversely corresponding change in the second movement from *Poco Adagio* to *Andante sostenuto*, had been instituted already by the time of the Munich performance on 15 November 1876 can be inferred from an anonymous review appearing in the *Allgemeine musikalische Zeitung* 12 (1877), col. 10. On the question of tempo in the third movement, see also Fritz Simrock's comment to Rudolf von Beckerath in an unpublished letter of 1 February 1878: "A propos des Allegretto grazioso aus der c-moll (1. Symphonie op. 68): die Bezeichnung ist falsch . . . Der Satz wird von Brahms selbst durchaus Andantino genommen" ("A propos the Allegretto grazioso of the C Minor [First Symphony, Op. 68]: the marking is false . . . Brahms himself took the movement Andantino throughout.") (Hamburg, Staats- und Universitätsbibliothek, Brahms-Archiv, Signatur 1969.3055).

27 See S. T. M. Newman, "The Slow Movement of Brahms's First Symphony: A Reconstruction of the Version First Performed Prior to Publication," *Music Review* 9 (1948), 4–12; Robert Pascall, "Brahms's First Symphony Slow Movement: The Initial Performing Version," *Musical Times* 122 (1981), 664–7; and Frithjof Haas, "Die Erstfassung des langsamen Satzes der ersten Sinfonie von Johannes Brahms," *Die Musikforschung* 36 (1983), 200–11. Haas includes a piano score of this early version; an edition in full score has recently appeared in Robert Pascall, *Brahms's First Symphony Andante – The Initial Performing Version: Commentary and Realisation*, Papers in Musicology, No. 2 (Department of Music, University of Nottingham, 1992). The string parts are owned by the Gesellschaft der Musikfreunde, Vienna.

28 *Schumann–Brahms Briefe*, II, 93.

29 Newman, "The Slow Movement of Brahms's First Symphony," 11; Margit L. McCorkle, "The Role of Trial Performances for Brahms's Orchestral and Large Choral Works: Sources and Circumstances," in *Brahms Studies: Analytical and Historical Perspectives*, ed. George S. Bozarth (Oxford, 1990), 316n; Raymond Knapp, "Brahms's Revisions Revisited," *Musical Times* 129 (1988), 584–8.

30 Because of severe cropping, all that remains visible of the second paste-over is a rejected five-measure version of the third movement's final six measures. Both paste-overs were made in the second half of October, at which time the score of Op. 67 was made ready for publication (see *Briefwechsel*, VI, 131; *Briefwechsel*, X, 14). This autograph was recently acquired by Robert Owen Lehman and is now on loan at the Pierpont Morgan Library, New York.

31 The one exception follows in the final complete system of the manuscript, which shows a rejected version of the link to A″ at m. 85 (m. 67 of the published text), whereby the main

theme is approached with a version of the ascending lines played by flute and clarinet in a slightly later lead-back to the head motif (cf. mm. 92–3 of the initial performing version and mm. 93–4 of the published text). Unfortunately, it is impossible to make much of the handful of note-heads that are barely visible immediately below this adumbration; the remainder of the sketch was lost to cropping.

32 Knapp's speculation evidently was prompted by a desire to reconcile the extant music with the composer's remarks to Dessoff at the time when he sent the scores of the middle movements. But Brahms's report of "a drastic shortening," appearing in a typically wry and obscure letter, probably concerned only the third movement. Indeed, as we have seen, when Clara later compared the original and the initial performing versions, she referred not to any "shortening" of the former but merely to an "alteration"; about the third movement, on the other hand, she complained that its ending was "altogether too short."

33 *Brahms und Simrock*, 88; *Briefwechsel*, X, 16. Arrangements for performances in Leipzig and Breslau (23 January 1877) can be followed in *Briefwechsel*, III, 140–1 and 209–11. Brahms had already promised Joachim that he could conduct the work in Cambridge, when, on 7 March 1877, he was to be awarded an honorary doctorate in music from the University; see *Briefwechsel*, VI, 131. Brahms had been unwilling to cross the Channel himself and thus made himself ineligible to claim the doctorate that had been intended also for him.

34 *Brahms und Simrock*, 96–7. The two London performances were scheduled only after Joachim's arrival in England and the second took place only after he had returned to Berlin; see *Briefwechsel*, VI, 132–6.

35 *Briefwechsel*, X, 29; *Brahms und Simrock*, 98.

36 When Brahms sent Simrock four books of songs in April 1877 he directed that they be published as Opp. 69–72, adding "Op. 68 we want to save f[or] t[he] s[ymphony]." (*Briefwechsel*, X, 26). On the subsequent preparation and delivery of the engraver's model, see *Briefwechsel*, X, 32–6; and *Brahms und Simrock*, 100.

37 See *Briefwechsel*, X, 37–50. Brahms made one last change in tempo, involving the coda of the first movement, only after witnessing the second Viennese performance (December 1878), after which he requested Simrock to replace *Poco sostenuto* at the end with *Meno Allegro* "because *Poco sostenuto* ... will be misunderstood and taken at the same tempo as in the introduction"; see *Briefwechsel*, X, 100.

38 *Brahms und Simrock*, 111–12.

39 *Briefwechsel*, X, 54–6.

3 Structure and meaning in the first movement

1 Joseph Joachim on Brahms's First Symphony (Fall 1877), quoted in Rudorff, "Johannes Brahms: Erinnerungen und Betrachtungen," 83.

2 Kalbeck, *Brahms*, I, 235.

3 Knapp, "Brahms's Revisions Revisited," 588.

4 Musgrave, *The Music of Brahms*, rev. edn (Oxford, 1994), 132; see also *idem*, "Die Erste Symphonie von Johannes Brahms: Stilistische und strukturelle Synthese," in *Probleme der Symphonischen Tradition im 19. Jahrhundert*, ed. Siegfried Kross and Marie Luise Maintz (Tutzing, 1990), 538–9.

5 By 1862 Brahms had under his belt already a number of other driving essays in C minor, in one of which – the scherzo of the so-called F–A–E Sonata for Violin and Piano, WoO 2 (1853) – he had even incorporated the "fate rhythm"; others include the scherzi of the Piano Quartet in G Minor, Op. 25, and Piano Quartet in C Minor, Op. 60.

6 Giselher Schubert, "Themes and Double Themes: The Problem of the Symphonic in Brahms," *19th-Century Music* 18 (1994), 15.

7 Raymond Knapp, "A Review of Norrington's Brahms," *American Brahms Society Newsletter* 9 (1993), 6.

8 *Briefwechsel*, III, 141; Litzmann, *Clara Schumann*, III, 340, 347. Along the same lines, after witnessing a rehearsal of the piece in Vienna in December 1876, Brahms's friend Theodor Billroth admitted to Eduard Hanslick his antipathy toward the "Faustian" first movement, with its "longwinded" rhythm, harmonies of "unpleasant effrontery," and general mood of "irritating *Sehnsucht*" (*Billroth und Brahms im Briefwechsel*, ed. Otto Gottlieb-Billroth [Berlin and Vienna, 1935], 228, n. 1).

9 Rudorff, "Johannes Brahms: Erinnerungen und Betrachtungen," 83.

10 Kalbeck, *Brahms*, III, 99. Knapp, "Brahms and the Problem of the Symphony," I, 105–6, n. 23. Presumably Brahms was familiar with Bach's use of "Ermuntre dich" in the *Christmas Oratorio* (with the text "Brich an, o schönes Morgenlicht") and in Cantata No. 43 (with the text "Du Lebensfürst, Herr Jesu Christ"); these works appeared in the Bach-Gesellschaft-Ausgabe in 1856 and 1860, respectively.

11 As noted by Musgrave, *Music of Brahms*, 138–40. See also Eric Sams, "Did Schumann Use Ciphers?" *Musical Times* 106 (1965), 584–91; Sams, "Brahms and His Clara Themes," *Musical Times* 112 (1971), 432–4; and David Brodbeck, "The Brahms–Joachim Counterpoint Exchange; or, Robert, Clara, and 'the Best Harmony between Jos. and Joh.,'" in *Brahms Studies*, vol. I, ed. David Brodbeck (Lincoln, Nbr., 1994), 69–72.

12 Among other relevant studies of Brahms's variations, see Constantin Floros, *Brahms und Bruckner: Studien zur musikalischen Exegetik* (Wiesbaden, 1980), 115–43; Oliver Neighbour, "Brahms and Schumann: Two Opus Nines and Beyond," *19th-Century Music* 7 (1983/84), 266–70; and Hermann Danuser, "Aspekte einer Hommage-Komposition. Zu Brahms' Schumann-Variationen op. 9," in *Brahms Analysen, Referate der Kieler Tagung 1983*, ed. Friedhelm Krummacher and Wolfgang Steinbeck (Kasse, 1984), 91–106. The "chorale theme" in Brahms's development also has certain points of contact with Schumann's theme (compare Examples 3.2a and 3.3b). Not only do the two themes (in G♭ major and F♯ minor, respectively) trace a generally similar shape (though, to be sure, Schumann's theme is lacking the distinctive opening upper neighbor-note figure of Brahms's theme, which might well have derived instead from the beginning of the transition, mm. 89ff.); they also show similar continuations. Schumann follows his initial phrase with a varied repetition that tonicizes the mediant (A major), a plan that Brahms likewise follows beginning in m. 242, when he too sets his theme in F♯ minor.

13 *Schumann–Brahms Briefe*, I, 198.

14 Sams, "Brahms and His Clara Themes," 434.

15 Kalbeck, *Brahms*, I, 153.

16 See Albert Dietrich's remarks in "Fragebogen für Herrn Hofkapellmeister Albert Dietrich," ed. Max Kalbeck, transcribed in Musikantiquariat Hans Schneider, *Katalog 100. Johannes Brahms: Leben und Werk, seine Freunde und seine Zeit* (Tutzing, 1964), 12: "I have a clear recollection from the y[ear] 1855 of the beginnings of a very somber piano quartet and of a very melodic and expressive second theme, which my friend Dr. H[ermann] Deiters also recognized again later in the Third Piano Quartet (C minor)." See also Clara Schumann's reference in her letter to Joachim of 28 March 1855 to "a magnificent first movement of a piano quartet" (quoted in Hofmann, "Johannes Brahms im Spiegel der Korrespondenz Clara Schumanns," 48). On the protracted compositional process of the work, see James Webster, "The C sharp minor Version of Brahms's Op. 60," *Musical Times* 121 (1980), 89–93; Webster, who evidently had not read Dietrich's recollection and did not know of the existence of Clara's letter to Joachim, incorrectly assumed that the work dated from 1856, when it entered Brahms's own correspondence with the violinist. For Brahms's subsequent verbal allusions to *Werther* in connection to this quartet, see Kalbeck, *Brahms*, III, 12; *Billroth und Brahms*, 211; *Briefwechsel*, vols. IX–X: *Johannes Brahms: Briefe an P. J. Simrock und Fritz Simrock*, ed. Max Kalbeck, 2 vols. (1917), IX, 200–201; and *Briefwechsel*, XIII: *Johannes Brahms im Briefwechsel mit Th. Wilhelm Engelmann*, ed. Julius Röntgen (1918), 22–5.

17 See Schumann's entry in the so-called marriage diaries from March 1841: "With a dear

gentle wife things go smoothly. Honestly, my next symphony shall be named 'Clara' and I will portray her in it with flutes, oboes, and harps" (*The Marriage Diaries of Robert & Clara Schumann: From Their Wedding Day through the Russia Trip*, ed. Gerd Nauhaus, trans. Peter Ostwald [Boston, 1993], 68–9). The reference here is to the first version of Schumann's Fourth Symphony, which dates from the spring of 1841, and whose autograph was one of Brahms's proudest possessions.

18 Michael Musgrave, projecting Kalbeck's notion over the entire work, has described the composition as Brahms's own "Clara Symphony" ("Brahms's First Symphony: Thematic Coherence and its Secret Origin," *Musical Analysis* 2 [1983], 117–33); and Robert Fink, ("Desire, Repression & Brahms's First Symphony, 97") likewise finds autobiographical significance in a piece that he believes to be "symbolically dominated by repressive struggles for control over transgressive desire." Musgrave scarcely addresses the question of genesis, however, and Fink, whose case rests largely on certain similarities between Brahms's *Schicksalsmotiv* and the famous chromatic beginning of Wagner's Prelude to *Tristan und Isolde*, implicitly rejects any dating before January 1860, when the prelude was published. In an older tradition, in which Kalbeck's tentative dating of 1855 is accepted uncritically, are works such as Alfred von Ehrmann, *Johannes Brahms: Weg, Werk und Welt* (Leipzig, 1933), 269–71; Hans Joachim Moser, "Zur Sinndeutung der Brahms'schen c-moll-Symphonie," in his *Musik in Zeit und Raum: Ausgewählte Abhandlungen* (Berlin, 1960), 220–3; and Alexander L. Ringer, "'Ende gut alles gut': Bemerkungen zu zwei Finalsätzen von Johannes Brahms und Gustav Mahler," in *Neue Musik und Tradition: Festschrift Rudolf Stephan zum 65. Geburtstag*, ed. Josef Kuckertz, Helga de la Motte-Haber, Christian Martin Schmidt, and Wilhelm Seidel (Laaber, 1990), 297–309.

19 Kalbeck, *Brahms*, I, 233–7; III, 92–3. Fink follows Kalbeck's interpretation and goes so far as to characterize the "Frei aber froh" motto as being "gender-separatist" ("Desire, Repression & Brahms's First Symphony," 80).

20 See Michael Musgrave, "*Frei aber Froh:* A Reconsideration," *19th-Century Music* 3 (1979/80), 251–8. One might add that during the time of Brahms's involvement with Clara Schumann he was neither very free nor very happy.

21 Reynolds, "A Choral Symphony by Brahms?" 7–8, 21. Brahms's use of the "Clara cipher" is discussed at length in Musgrave, "Brahms's First Symphony," 125–30, and *Music of Brahms*, 138–40.

22 *Schumann–Brahms Briefe*, I, 100. Brahms's wish to hear the *Manfred* music in Clara's company soon came to pass. Georg Dietrich Otten performed the work in Hamburg on 21 April 1855, and Brahms traveled with Clara from Düsseldorf to be in attendance.

23 The relevant passage from the letter in question, which Brahms left unsigned (out of "shame" for having let Schubring's request to see new works go unanswered for too long), reads: "The music is the one answer [to your last letter], and at the same time my signature, since I cannot properly sign this one at the end. You will certainly discover the name and proceed to your writing." *Briefwechsel*, VIII: *Briefe an Joseph Viktor Widmann, Ellen und Ferdinand Vetter, Adolf Schubring*, ed. Max Kalbeck (1915), 187. For a fuller discussion, see Brodbeck, "The Brahms–Joachim Counterpoint Exchange," 73–5.

24 Rudorff, "Johannes Brahms: Erinnerungen und Betrachtungen," 83.

25 Thus these comments by an anonymous reviewer of the first performance of the symphony in Boston (3 January 1878): "Schumann's 'Manfred' music was in our mind more hauntingly than any other through the whole first movement." *Dwight's Journal of Music* 37 (19 January 1878), 166.

26 It is no wonder, then, that the following descriptions of the two works seem almost interchangable: "The greatest achievement of Schumann as a composer of programme music, and indeed as a composer generally, is the overture to Manfred. It is one of the most original and grandest orchestral compositions ever conceived, one of the most powerful, but at the same time one of the most sombre, soul-portraits ever painted. The sombreness is nowhere

relieved, although contrast to the dark brooding and the surging agitation of despair is obtained by the tender, longing, regretful recollection of Astarte, the destroyed beloved one" (Frederick Niecks, *Programme Music in the The Last Four Centuries: A Contribution to the History of Musical Expression* [London, 1906], 209–10); and "The oppressed, haunted mood of crisis that dominates the first movement has resulted in a restlessness of musical idiom such as can probably not be found anywhere else in Brahms's music. It is true that the opening movement of the D minor Concerto was born in a similarly tragic vein, but there are after all extended interludes of lyrical peace in it. These are completely lacking in the first movement of the symphony, in which one brief thematic episode (second subject) for the oboe hardly affords more than a fleeting moment of quiet" (Hans Gal, *Johannes Brahms: His Work and Personality*, trans. Joseph Stein [1963; rpt. edn, Westport, Conn., 1977], 207).

27 I use the term "misreading" here in the sense in which it has been popularized by Harold Bloom, who argues that "strong poets" purposely misinterpret the works of their predecessors in a kind of Oedipal power struggle to find their own voice. Among other studies, see Harold Bloom, *A Map of Misreading* (New York, 1975).

28 James Webster, "Brahms's *Tragic Overture:* The Form of Tragedy," in *Brahms: Biographical, Documentary, and Analytical Studies*, ed. Robert Pascall (Cambridge, 1983), 119–20.

29 As we have seen, Musgrave (*Music of Brahms*, p. 132) finds another possible model for Brahms's "motto-like introduction to the main allegro" in Beethoven's Piano Sonata in E♭ (*Les adieux*), Op. 81a (mm. 17–20), whereas Fink ("Desire, Repression & Brahms's First Symphony," 79–81) relates the same idea to the chromatically charged opening of the *Tristan* Prelude. But even if the *Schicksalsmotiv* thus spins a kind of allusive web involving formidable works by Beethoven, Schumann, and Wagner, the *Manfred* thread would seem to claim priority.

30 For a convenient résumé and discussion, see Kenneth Hull, "Brahms the Allusive" (Ph.D. dissertation, Princeton University, 1989), 14–22.

31 Overstating, in my view, the palpable links between this melody and the substance of the opening material, Robert Fink argues that the movement presents no real "second theme," at least none that might, in accordance with recent gendered readings of sonata form, be set against the movement's masculine protagonist as a threatening feminine Other. Fink reads the piece instead as "a struggle for sexual control not between male and female, but within one male psyche, divided against itself" ("Desire, Repression & Brahms's First Symphony," 83). In this reading, then, Brahms's obsessive treatment of the motto is likened, not to guilt over past transgressions, but to an ever-present threatening sexual desire that must, in Freudian terms, constantly be repressed.

4 The middle movements

1 Letter of 22 November 1876 from Hermann Levi to Clara Schumann (Litzmann, *Clara Schumann*, III, 343).

2 It has often been remarked that Brahms's choice of E major as the key for the slow movement of a C minor cycle derives from Beethoven's Piano Concerto in C Minor, Op. 37. Recently Christian Martin Schmidt has argued that the use of A♭ major for the third movement might, at the same time, derive from Beethoven's other concerto in C, the Triple Concerto, Op. 56, whose middle movement likewise is in the flat submediant; see Christian Martin Schmidt, *Johannes Brahms* (Stuttgart, 1994), 47.

3 The first phrase (mm. 1–4) recalls also the main theme of Beethoven's Piano Concerto in C Minor, as perhaps Dessoff had recognized when in October 1876 he wrote to the composer that the initial four measures "might be by someone other than Brahms."

4 The slow movements of both the Third and Fourth symphonies are marked by similar "digressive" allusions, in which, as Robert Bailey has put it, Brahms seems "for a moment . . . to depart from the context of the movement, bringing in a short section apparently different

from anything else in the movement, and then allowing the original context to resume" ("Musical Language and Structure in the Third Symphony," in *Brahms Studies: Analytical and Historical Perspectives*, ed. George S. Bozarth [Oxford, 1991], 405). In the Third Symphony the composer alludes to the "Immolation Scene" at the end of Wagner's *Götterdämmerung*. In the Fourth Symphony, allusion is made to the slow movement of Beethoven's Fifth Symphony; see Kenneth Hull, "Allusive Irony in Brahms's Fourth Symphony," in *Brahms Studies*, vol. II, ed. David Brodbeck [Lincoln, Nbr., forthcoming]).

5   The three-page autograph of this ending, which Brahms acquired from Carl Tausig in 1864, is one of several pieces of Wagneriana to be found in the composer's estate (Vienna, Gesellschaft der Musikfreunde).

6   As noted by Fink ("Desire, Repression & Brahms's First Symphony," 96), although with reference, not to the Concert Ending of the Prelude, but to the *Liebestod* itself.

7   Richard Pohl, *Musikalisches Wochenblatt* 7 (1876), 657.

8   The movement has occasionally been analysed as a five-part rondo form (ABA'CA"), however; see *Symphony Number One [in C Minor], by Johannes Brahms, Opus 68, For Piano Two Hands* (Analytic Symphony Series, No. 20), ed. Percy Goetschus (Philadelphia, n.d.); and Louise Cuyler, *The Symphony* (New York, 1973), 115.

9   Tovey, *Essays in Musical Analysis*, I, 90.

10   A similar concern for continuity between sections can be noticed in passages such as mm. 62ff., where a sixteenth-note figure from the preceding section (derived from the main theme) serves as a background against which the main theme itself is reintroduced.

11   Julius Harrison, "Johannes Brahms (1833–97)," in *The Symphony*, ed. Robert Simpson, 2 vols. (New York, 1966), I, 324.

12   Knapp, "Brahms's Revisions Revisited," 588.

5 Structure and meaning in the last movement

1   Kalbeck, *Brahms*, III, 111.

2   Hans Gal, *Johannes Brahms: His Work and Personality*, 140–1.

3   Tovey, *Essays in Musical Analysis*, I, 92. Actually, as we have seen, many gestures can be traced back to the Allegretto.

4   Knapp, "Brahms and the Problem of the Symphony," I, 18–23.

5   Tovey, *Essays in Musical Analysis*, I, 93; Musgrave, *Music of Brahms*, 133–4.

6   Among other sources for the "jackass" anecdote, see Kalbeck, *Brahms*, III, 109n; and Rudorff, "Johannes Brahms: Erinnerungen und Betrachtungen," 83.

7   Henschel, *Personal Recollections of Johannes Brahms*, 33; *Briefwechsel*, X, 30, 32.

8   *Neue Zeitschrift für Musik* 73 (12 January 1877), 27.

9   Tappert's review, from which we shall quote at greater length in Chapter 6, appeared in the *Allgemeine Deutsche Musikzeitung* 4 (16 November 1877), 363. The anonymous American review was carried in both the New York *World* (23 December 1877) and *Dwight's Journal of Music* (5 January 1878) and has recently been reprinted in the *American Brahms Society Newsletter* 10 (1992), 7–8.

10   "Nehmen wir einmal den Fall, Du hättest das Thema nicht als Scarlattisches bezeichnet und irgend ein dummer Leipziger Prophet hätte es spontan 'als Plagiat' entdeckt; welch ein Halloh und Geflüstere wäre erfolgt! Nun Du durch die Bezeichnung 'Scarlatti' den Anklang als *beabsichtigt* erklärt hast, kann Dir niemand etwas anhaben. Wie wäre es, wenn Du es bei dem Hauptthema des Schlußsatzes der C-m[oll] Symphonie ebenso machtest und in Partitur und Klavierauszug Dich dazu bekenntest, daß ein Hommage à Beethoven et Schumann *beabsichtigt* wurde? Du glaubst nicht, was die kleine Beethovensche Reminiszenz aus der Neunten Dir in Leipzig auf dem [illegible] zum Verbrechen angerechnet worden ist; hätte nun Bernsdorf oder Konsorten gar noch gefunden, da auch die erste Hälfte des Themas fast

wörtlich das (von Andern, nicht aber von mir) vergessene Schumann/Becker Rheinlied ist, so wäre es dem [?] Bernsdorf völlig klar geworden, daß Du ein ganz unfähiger Hervorbringer von epigonischen Erzeugnissen 5ter Ordnung bist. Allen diesen albernen Schreibern stopfst Du mit einem [illegible] das Maul, wenn Du darüber schreibst: ⌊*Schumann*⌋ ⌊*Beethoven*⌋. Solltest Du Schumanns Rheinlied nicht kennen, so setze ich Dir hier den Anfang hin: [mus. ex.]. Vielleicht trifft Dich dieser Brief gerade beim Correkturlesen des 4ten Satzes." Hamburg, Staats- und Universitätsbibliothek Carl von Ossietzky, Signatur 1965.2201.

11 *Briefwechsel*, XVI, 60. Several years later, in January 1882, the composer told Hans von Bülow his opinion that the ascending stepwise bass of Bach's movement would, if suitably modified with some chromaticism, make a good point of departure for a *Sinfoniesatz* (Siegfried Ochs, *Geschehenes, Gesehenes* [Leipzig, 1922], 199–200). As is well known, Brahms eventually realized this potential in the ciacona finale of his Fourth Symphony.

12 There can be little question that Brahms kept Bach in mind during the summer in which he composed the waltzes and worked on the symphonic finale. Upon returning to Vienna in September 1874 he sent Spitta a query concerning the latter's transcription of a passage from the last chorus of "Nach dir, Herr, verlanget mich" (*Briefwechsel*, XVI, 62); a grateful Spitta, in turn, took note of this advice in the subsequent English translation of his biography (*Johann Sebastian Bach: His Work and Influence on the Music of Germany, 1685–1750*, trans. Clara Bell and J. A. Fuller-Maitland, 3 vols. [London, 1880], I, 446n.).

13 Friedrich Chrysander, [Review of the Hamburg performance of 18 January 1878], *Allgemeine musikalische Zeitung* 13 (1878), col. 94. Much more recently (though in the same spirit), Richard Taruskin has suggested that Brahms's allusion to the choral theme within a purely instrumental context "corrected the wrong turn that Beethoven had taken, with what dire results for the Master's corybantic followers." Richard Taruskin, "Resisting the Ninth," *19th-Century Music* 12 (1988/89), 247.

14 See Johannes Brahms, *1. Sinfonie c-Moll, op. 68*, with introduction and analysis by Giselher Schubert, 2nd edn (Mainz, 1988), 67–73; Reinhold Brinkmann, *Johannes Brahms, Die Zweite Symphonie, Späte Idylle* (Munich, 1990), 19–23; revised and translated as *Late Idyll: The Second Symphony of Johannes Brahms*, trans. Peter Palmer (Cambridge, Mass., 1995), 33–44; and Schubert, "Themes and Double Themes," 22–3n. See also Brinkmann, "Brahms und die 'Mächte der Massen.' Über Struktur und Idee der 1. Symphonie," in *Berliner Philharmonisches Orchester: Philharmonische Programme 1983/84*, No. 40 (19–20 June 1984), 815–25. Among other analyses of the last movement, see Bruno Stäblein, "Die motivische Arbeit im Finale der ersten Brahms-Sinfonie," *Das Musikleben* 2 (1949), 69–72; and Knapp, "Brahms and the Problem of the Symphony," I, 145–53.

15 James Hepokoski, "Fiery-Pulsed Libertine or Domestic Hero? Strauss's *Don Juan* Revisited," in *Richard Strauss: New Perspectives on the Composer and His Work*, ed. Bryan Gilliam (Durham, N.C., 1992), 143. The ensuing discussion draws also from *idem, Sibelius: Symphony No. 5* (Cambridge, 1993), 5–7, 94–5n.

16 Among other discussions of this Brahmsian formal type, see Robert Pascall, "Some Special Uses of Sonata Form by Brahms," *Soundings* 4 (1974), 58–63; and John Daverio, "From 'Concertante Rondo' to 'Lyric Sonata': A Commentary on Brahms's Reception of Mozart," in *Brahms Studies*, 111–38.

17 Brinkmann, *Late Idyll*, 34.

18 *Ibid.*, 45.

19 See above, note 9.

20 See Constantin Floros, *Gustav Mahler II: Mahler und die Symphonik des 19. Jahrhunderts in neuer Deutung, Zur Grundlegung einer zeitgemäßen musikalischen Exegetik* (Wiesbaden, 1977), 129–30.

21 Musgrave, "Die Erste Symphonie von Johannes Brahms," 541–3.

22 For two important studies of Schumann's symphony, see Anthony Newcomb, "Once More Between Absolute and Program Music: Schumann's Second Symphony," *19th-Century*

Music 7 (1983/84), 233–50; and Linda Correll Roesner, "Tonal Strategy and Poetic Content in Schumann's C-Major Symphony, Op. 61," in *Probleme der symphonischen Tradition im 19. Jahrhundert*, 295–306.

23 On Brahms's awareness of this allusion, see his letter to Clara Schumann of 8 December 1855 (*Schumann–Brahms Briefe*, I, 160).

24 See Hans Kohlhase, "Brahms und Mendelssohn: Strukturelle Parallelen in der Kammermusik für Streicher," in *Brahms und seine Zeit: Symposium Hamburg 1983*, ed. Constantin Floros, Hans Joachim Marx, and Peter Petersen (Laaber, 1984), 67–8.

25 Brahms's allusion to Bach, then, comes in two stages: first to the bass line, then to the compositional technique.

26 This allusion evidently was noticed by the reviewer for the *Times* of the first London performance (31 March 1877): "We have reminiscences here and there, it is true, of the theme upon which the *finale* of Beethoven's Choral Symphony is constructed, and of much of the contrapuntal working out of the last movement in Mozart's so-styled 'Jupiter'" (quoted in *Dwight's Journal of Music* 37 [28 April 1877], 10).

27 The source of this "combined reference" is found in the strings' continuing scalar passage in sixteenth notes, which is itself an outgrowth of a clearer "combined reference" in the exposition (mm. 107ff.). In Musgrave's view, this idea ultimately can be traced back to the "Clara cipher" that had figured so prominently in the opening Allegro; see Musgrave, "Brahms's First Symphony," 123, and *Music of Brahms*, 137–8.

28 Spitta, *Bach*, I, 456.

29 M. H. Abrams, *Natural Supernaturalism: Tradition and Revolution in Romantic Literature* (New York, 1971), 187–8. For a complementary reading of Brahms's use in the motet "Warum ist das Licht gegeben," Op. 74. No. 1 (1877), of material related to Bach's *Actus tragicus*, see Daniel Beller-McKenna, "The Great 'Warum?': Job, Christ, and Bach in a Motet," *19th-Century Music* 19 (1995/96), 231–51.

30 Arnold Whittall, *Romantic Music: A Concise History from Schubert to Sibelius* (London, 1987), 166.

31 Litzmann, *Clara Schumann*, III, 349.

32 Quoted in *Dwight's Journal of Music* 37 (2 February 1878), 171.

6 Early reception

1 Letter of 26 November 1876 from Brahms to Otto Dessoff, in *Briefwechsel*, XVI, 153.

2 Letter of 25 September 1877 from Hans von Bülow to Jessie Laussot, in Hans von Bülow, *Briefe*, 7 vols., ed. Marie von Bülow (Leipzig, 1895-1908), V (1904), 454.

3 Letter of 2 February 1878 from Richard Wagner to an unnamed correspondent, in *The Letters of Richard Wagner*, ed. John Burk (New York, 1950), 657.

4 Eduard Hanslick, [Review of the first performance in Vienna, 17 December 1876], *Neue Freie Presse* (28 December 1876), 1; translation from Eduard Hanslick, *Music Criticisms 1846–99*, trans. and ed. Henry Pleasants (Baltimore, 1950), 125.

5 Walter Frisch, *Brahms: The Four Symphonies* (New York, in press), Ch. 7; I am grateful to Professor Frisch for allowing me to read his work in typescript. See also Giselher Schubert's discussion of reception issues in Brahms, *1. Sinfonie*, 36–51.

6 For a useful discussion of the early journalistic reception of the First Symphony, drawing upon some eighty-five reviews in daily newspapers and musical periodicals, see Angelika Hortstmann, *Untersuchungen zur Brahms-Rezeption der Jahre 1860–1880* (Hamburg, 1986), 248–79. For reproductions of some of these reviews, see Brahms, *1. Sinfonie* (ed. Schubert), 27–33; Knapp, "Brahms and the Problem of the Symphony," 536–45; and Fuchs, "Zeitgenössische Aufführungen der Ersten Symphonie."

7 [Wilhelm Lübke,] in *Allgemeine Zeitung* [Augsburg], No. 316 (11 November 1876), 4818.

8 Richard Pohl, in *Musikalisches Wochenblatt* 7 (17 November 1876), 657. For Max Kalbeck's fanciful poetic "program" of the symphony, see Appendix 1.

9 For a survey of Viennese critical opinion concerning the First Symphony, see Fuchs, "Zeitgenössische Aufführungen der Ersten Symphonie," 167–86.

10 Hanslick, *Music Criticisms*, 127–8.

11 Hermann Zopff, in *Neue Zeitschrift für Musik* 73 (16 March 1877), 81–3; [Eduard Bernsdorff,] in *Signale für die musikalische Welt* 35/7 (January 1877), 100; translated in *Dwight's Journal of Music* (22 December 1877), 150.

12 Carl Kipke, in *Musikalisches Wochenblatt* 8 (26 January 1877), 68.

13 Von Bülow's letter to Jessie Laussot is cited above, note 2; his letter to Brahms of 2 October 1877 has recently been published in Hans von Bülow, *Die Briefe an Johannes Brahms*, ed. Hans-Joachim Hinrichsen (Tutzing, 1994), 29.

14 "Possierlich ist es, daß auch Beethoven im Schlußsatze seiner Neunten (die der Zehnten nicht nachsteht) – wie ich Dir schon in Leipzig einmal erwähnte, Mendelssohns 'Es ist bestimmt in Gottes Rat' und Papagenos 'Denn alle Vögel sind ja mein' copuliert hat." Unpublished letter in Hamburg, Staats- und Universitätsbibliothek Carl von Ossietzky, Signatur 1965.2201.

15 Reprinted in Hans von Bülow, *Ausgewählte Schriften 1850–1896* (Leipzig, 1896), 369–72.

16 Quoted in *Dwight's Journal of Music* (2 February 1878), 171. Somewhat more diplomatically, another anonymous reviewer wrote: "We venture, however, at this stage of our acquaintance with the Brahms symphony to express a doubt ... that this work demonstrates its author's right to a place beside or near Beethoven, or that it entitles his admirers to disregard the claims of Mendelssohn and Schumann in ranking this composition as the greatest since the Ninth Symphony" (*ibid.*).

17 Wilhelm Tappert, "Aus dem Konzertsaal," *Allgemeine Deutsche Musikzeitung* 4 (16 November 1877), 363–4.

18 Pascall, *Brahms's First Symphony Andante*, 11.

19 Friedrich Chrysander, in *Allgemeine musikalische Zeitung* 13 (1878), col. 94.

20 See *Cosima Wagner's Diaries*, ed. Martin Gregor-Dallin and Dietrich Mack, trans. Geoffrey Skelton, 2 vols. (New York, 1978–80), II, 25, 154. The editors' remark in the commentary on the first of these entries (*ibid.*, 1022) that Wagner's reference was to the Second Symphony cannot be correct; the First appeared in print in October 1877, the Second only in August 1878. On Wagner's acquisition of the scores, see his letter of 2 February 1878 (as cited above in note 3, the editor of which makes the same mistake regarding the identity of the symphony in question). Wagner's reference to Brahms's "tremolando theme" suggests that the passage in question was the slow introduction to the finale, where the initial appearance of the alphorn theme is supported by quiet tremolando figures in the upper strings (mm. 30ff.).

21 Wagner, *Gesammelte Schriften und Dichtungen*, 3rd edn, 10 vols. (Leipzig, 1887–8), vol. X (1888), 137–51, see 148, 150.

22 *Ibid.*, 152–75.

23 *Ibid.*, 176–93. The following passages are drawn from pp. 181–3. Kipke's essay is quoted above, pp. 83–4; Wagner would surely have known this review, since it appears in the same issue as his own open letter "An die geehrten Vorstände der Richard Wagner-Verein" (*Musikalisches Wochenblatt* 8 [26 January 1877], 61–3). Wagner's parody is most readily recognized in his use of the biting phrase "von Gernwollen und Nichtkönnen," which brings to mind Kipke's notion that in the finale of the First Symphony Brahms had become trapped in an incongruity between his aspiration and ability (*Wollen und Können*). Wagner's snide references to "Hungarian" and "Scottish" works, on the other hand, can probably be connected to Joachim and Mendelssohn, respectively, both of whom figure in von Bülow's open letter in the *Signale*. See also Klaus Kropfinger, *Wagner and Beethoven: Richard Wagner's Reception of Beethoven*, trans. Peter Palmer (Cambridge, 1991), 251–3.

24 For an important study on the "sociology" of Brahms's symphonies, see Margaret Notley,

"Brahms as Liberal: Genre, Style, and Politics in Late-19th-Century Vienna," *19th-Century Music* 17 (1993/94), 107–23.

25 Letter of 10 December 1876, in *Billroth und Brahms*, 225–6.

26 J. Peter Burkholder, "Brahms and Twentieth-Century Classical Music," *19th-Century Music* 8 (1984/85), 75–83 (here p. 81 is quoted). See also *idem*, "Museum Pieces: The Historicist Mainstream of the Last Hundred Years," *Journal of Musicology* 2 (1983), 115–34.

27 Letter of 3 August 1888 to Hans von Bronsart, in von Bülow, *Briefe*, VII (1908), 205.

Select bibliography

Brahms, Johannes. *1. Sinfonie c-Moll, op. 68*. Introduction and analysis by Giselher Schubert. 2nd edn Mainz, 1988.
   Symphonie Nr. 1 c-Moll opus 68. Neue Ausgabe sämtlicher Werke. Edited by Robert Pascall. Munich, 1996.
Brinkmann, Reinhold. *Johannes Brahms, Die Zweite Symphonie, Späte Idylle*. Munich, 1990. Revised and translated as *Late Idyll: The Second Symphony of Johannes Brahms*. Translated by Peter Palmer. Cambridge, Mass., 1995.
Brodbeck, David. "Brahms." In *The Nineteenth-Century Symphony*. Edited by D. Kern Holoman. New York, in press.
Clara Schumann–Johannes Brahms: Briefe aus den Jahren 1853–1896. Edited by Berthold Litzmann. 2 vols. Leipzig, 1927. Translated as *Letters of Clara Schumann and Johannes Brahms, 1853–1896*. 2 vols. 1927; rpt. New York, 1971.
Fink, Robert. "Desire, Repression & Brahms's First Symphony." *repercussions* 2 (1993), 75–103.
Frisch, Walter. *Brahms: The Four Symphonies*. New York, in press.
Fuchs, Ingrid. "Zeitgenössische Aufführungen der Ersten Symphonie Op. 68 von Johannes Brahms in Wien: Studien zur Wiener Brahms-Rezeption." In *Brahms-Kongress Wien 1983, Kongressbericht*, edited by Susanne Antonicek and Otto Biba, pp. 167–86. Tutzing, 1988.
Haas, Frithjof. "Die Erstfassung des langsamen Satzes der ersten Sinfonie von Johannes Brahms." *Die Musikforschung* 36 (1983), 200–11.
Harrison, Julius. *Brahms and His Four Symphonies*. London, 1939; rpt. New York, 1971.
Horstmann, Angelika. *Untersuchungen zur Brahms-Rezeption der Jahre 1860–1880*. Hamburg, 1986.
Johannes Brahms Briefwechsel. 19 vols. to date. 16 orig. vols. Rev. edns Berlin, 1912–22; repr. Tutzing, 1974. *Neue Folge*. 3 vols. to date. Tutzing, 1991–.
Kalbeck, Max. *Johannes Brahms*. Rev. edns 4 vols. in 8. Berlin, 1915–21; repr. Tutzing, 1976.
Knapp, Raymond. *Brahms and the Challenge of the Symphony*. New York, in press.
   "Brahms's Revisions Revisited." *Musical Times* 129 (1988), 584–8.
   "The Finale of Brahms's Fourth Symphony: The Tale of the Subject." *19th-Century Music* 13 (1989/90), 3–17.

"Brahms and the Problem of the Symphony: Romantic Image, Generic Conception, and Compositional Challenge." Ph. D. dissertation, Duke University, 1987.

Kross, Siegfried. "Brahms the Symphonist." In *Brahms: Biographical, Documentary, and Analytical Studies*, edited by Robert Pascall, pp. 125–45. Cambridge, 1983.

Litzmann, Berthold. *Clara Schumann: Ein Künstlerleben nach Tagebüchern und Briefen.* 3 vols. Leipzig, 1902–8.

MacDonald, Malcolm. *Brahms.* New York, 1990.

McCorkle, Margit L. "The Role of Trial Performances for Brahms's Orchestral and Large Choral Works: Sources and Circumstances." In *Brahms Studies: Analytical and Historical Perspectives*, edited by George S. Bozarth, pp. 295–328. Oxford, 1990.

Musgrave, Michael. "Brahms's First Symphony: Thematic Coherence and its Secret Origin." *Music Analysis* 2 (1983), 117–33.

"Die Erste Symphonie von Johannes Brahms: Stilistische und strukturelle Synthese." In *Probleme der Symphonischen Tradition im 19. Jahrhundert*, edited by Siegfried Kross and Marie Luise Maintz, pp. 537–44. Tutzing, 1990.

The Music of Brahms. [Revised edition.] Oxford, 1994.

Newman, S. T. M. "The Slow Movement of Brahms's First Symphony: A Reconstruction of the Version First Performed Prior to Publication." *Music Review* 9 (1948), 4–12.

Pascall, Robert. *Brahms's First Symphony Andante – The Initial Performing Version: Commentary and Realisation.* Papers in Musicology, No. 2. Department of Music, University of Nottingham, 1992.

Reynolds, Christopher. "A Choral Symphony by Brahms?" *19th-Century Music* 9 (1985/86), 3–25.

Tovey, Donald Francis. *Essays in Musical Analysis*, vol. I: *Symphonies.* London, 1948.

Wagner, Richard. *Gesammelte Schriften und Dichtungen.* 3rd edn 10 vols. Leipzig, 1887–8.

Index